AF699780

Towards a Political Economy of Information

Studies on the Information Economy

Roberto Verzola

ISBN 971-8741-24-0

Published by :
Foundation for Nationalist Studies, Inc.
38 Panay Avenue
Quezon City
Philippines

First Printing March 2004

Contents

Author's Note

This is a collection of pieces I have written over the past decade about the social implications of information and communications technologies (ICT).

Because the pieces are generally critical of the social impact of ICT, they might be useful to policy-makers who want to hear a second opinion before investing huge amounts in the new technologies, as well as to students and researchers who are interested in the negative impacts of science and technology on society.

I started working with digital technology around 1979, as a returning engineering student at the University of the Philippines. In 1981, I began a student project to design and assemble a microcomputer, with a Z80 microprocessor, 16-kilobyte memory, a converted B&W TV set for display (64 characters x 16 lines), and another converted tape recorder for storage. I finished a working model and graduated in 1982. I also submitted the project for funding by the National Science and Technology Authority (today's Department of Science and Technology). With the funding, I improved the design further and completed in 1984 the assembly of five prototypes and more than 20 programs in BASIC that showcased the capabilities of the machines. I've been told that this is probably the first microcomputer designed by a Filipino. At least, nobody has come forward so far with an earlier claim!

Everybody told me the design was my ticket to wealth, but I saw clearly that the industrial infrastructure in the Philippines was not ready for computer manufacturing. If we had to import the simplest components like resistors and capacitors, as well as the simplest tools like pliers and screwdrivers from Taiwan, how could we ever compete with imported brands? Even integrated circuits assembled locally, mostly in export processing zones, had to be exported first, and later imported again, before I could use them.

So, I concentrated on software. I worked with Ibon Databank and wrote a data retrieval program for them. We also explored other computer applications, like e-mail, which Ibon had by 1985. After Ibon, I set up a computer center for NGOs, People's Access, which became my platform for ICT advocacy. In 1986, I set up the Andromeda Bulletin Board System (BBS), one of the first in the Philippines. I used the BBS as a test bed to further explore the possibilities of the computer for communications, networking and democratization. In the process, I even wrote my own BBS program called Andro. With the support of the Philippine Development Alternatives Foundation, we used the software to set up a publicly-accessible BBS both in the Philippine Senate and Congress.

Throughout the 1980s and early 1990s, I pioneered in ICT advocacy. I introduced foundations, non-government organizations and social movements in the Philippines and in Southeast Asia to word processing, spreadsheet work, databases and, later, communications. Meanwhile, I also got involved in the campaign against the Bataan nuclear plant, the campaign for demand-side management, energy efficiency and renewable energies, the debt campaign, the campaign against GATT, and other issues.

In 1992, I turned the Andromeda BBS into an Internet e-mail server called the Email Center, which provided electronic mail services to environmental groups, women's groups, church groups, foundations, and similar groups and progressive individuals. I also got involved in environmental issues, including the campaign against genetically-engineered organisms in food and agriculture.

This book is the result of my intimate involvement with the technology, at its deepest level of hardware and software. It is about the role of the technology within a social and historical context.

From an advocate, I gradually turned into a skeptic and then a critic of the technology. I realized that I had been playing the same role as the missionaries of old. Despite their good intentions, they in fact laid the groundwork for changing mindsets, prying open local markets, and paving the way for foreign investments. I eventually realized that the computer and the Internet were a leading edge of globalization, bringing with them new forms of wealth accumulation, concentration, and neo-colonial enslavement.

I closed EMC down in 2000, when my Internet uplink decided to phase out UUCP, an older protocol which made low-cost emails possible. The pressure to provide full Internet access was pulling me towards commercial business operation. I decided to remain a social activist.

The pieces in this book are my contribution to the growing body of critical literature about the new ICTs and their impact particularly on developing countries, on industrial and pre-industrial societies and on traditional livelihoods. I had hesitated to publish these pieces into a book, because they lack the references required to meet the scholarship standards in some academic circles. The pieces are products of practical activist work more than scholarly theoretical research, written for the ordinary public more than an academic audience. However, I have been getting very encouraging comments from colleagues and friends about the unique insights that some of the pieces carry, convincing me to publish.

Because many chapters are actually stand-alone pieces which have earlier been published separately, I hope the reader will forgive the repetition of ideas and even paragraphs across some chapters.

It is not possible to list all who had helped and encouraged me along the way. But I must name a few: Jagdish Parikh, my long-time colleague and friend in Interdoc and the Asialink project, as well as others I closely worked with in the course of several Interdoc meetings we held in the 1980s and 1990s: Karen Banks of GreenNet UK; Leo Fernandez of IndiaLink, Michael Polman of Antenna Netherlands; Mario Mapanao of NCCP; Norbert Klein of Open Forum Cambodia; Susanna George and the women of Isis International; John Sayer of the Asia Monitor Resource Center; Tony Manipon; Andrew Garton; Peter Benjamin; Michael Gurstein;

Heimo Claasen; my brother Pio Jr./Jun, for keeping me on my toes with his counter-arguments; the Email Center subscribers who stuck with me to the end; grappling with what seemed to be the wrong end of a double-edged sword; and Letizia R. Constantino and Red Constantino, for publishing this book. A special mention goes to my wife Flor, for her support and understanding. Finally, my deepest gratitude goes to my parents Pio and Anastasia Verzola for everything.

To them, and to all the others who had encouraged me along the way, I dedicate this book.

Roberto Verzola
Quezon City, March 10, 2004

Part I. Information and Intellectual Property Rights

The potentials of information as a distinct commodity were already apparent in books, tapes and similar media. But they were fully realized only after the computer became a mass consumer product.

With the computer, the user acquired not only a very flexible means of "enjoying" information, but also a means of reproducing it. With digital technology, perfect reproduction of copies became a reality. Thus, the user also became a potential producer.

Part I focuses on conflicting attitudes towards information: as a good which, in the developing world, one naturally shares with others; and as a commodity of which, in the developed world, one claims ownership, for purposes of profit-making. The different attitudes reflect the emerging conflict over information between the developed economies which are trying to consolidate their early lead in information ownership and control, and the developing economies which are trying to use their access to easily-copied material to accelerate their own development.

This conflict manifests itself as an "offensive" by the U.S. and other information economies to impose on developing countries a strict regime of intellectual property rights (IPR) enforcement. Through this regime, they expand and consolidate their ownership and control over information. (Chapter 2)

By accusing developing countries of "piracy," the U.S. is trying to gain the high moral ground in the conflict. Yet, the U.S. itself freely copied British books and other publications in the 19th century (Chapter 3) and until today remains guilty of the worse practice of "pirating" intellectuals rather than intellectual property. (Chapter 4)

The international legal infrastructure which the U.S. chose to consolidate its superiority in the information sector is the General Agreement on Tariffs and Trade (GATT). This agreement is supposedly against protectionism but is highly protectionist over IPR. It is supposedly for free trade but includes major provisions that strengthen information monopolies. (Chapter 5)

With information emerging as a major commodity in its own right, three qualitatively distinct types of production sectors now exist, distinguished by the type of goods they deal with: living goods of the agriculture sector, non-living material goods of the industrial sector, and non-material goods of the information sector. The value-systems linked with each of the sectors are also different. (Chapter 6)

Part I ends with an initial analysis of the political economy of information. It looks at the unique features of information goods; how these features affect their production, distribution and consumption; ownership forms over information; the propertied classes of the information sector; and the relationship between information economies and older industrial and agriculture economies. (Chapter 7)

1. The miracle of the loaves

In those days when there again was a great crowd without anything to eat, he summoned the disciples and said, "My heart is moved with pity for the crowd, because they have been with me now for three days and have nothing to eat. If I send them away hungry to their homes, they will collapse on the way, and some of them have come a great distance."

His disciples answered him, "Where can anyone get enough bread to satisfy them here in this deserted place?"

Still he asked them, "How many loaves do you have?" "Seven," they replied. He ordered the crowd to sit down on the ground.

Then, taking the seven loaves he gave thanks, broke them, and gave them to his disciples to distribute, and they distributed them to the crowd. They also had a few fish. He said the blessing over them and ordered them distributed also.

They ate and were satisfied.

They picked up the fragments left over – seven baskets. There were about four thousand people.[1]

A version of this piece appeared on the NMCL Bulletin Board, *Vol. 10 No. 6 (March-April 1997), a bimonthly packet that consists of a four-page newsletter and five separate one-page pieces suitable for posting on a wall or a bulletin board. The* Bulletin Board *was published until 2001 by the National Movement for Civil Liberties and currently by the Foundation for Nationalist Studies.*

[1] *New Testament,* Mark, Ch. 8:1-9; see also Ch. 6:34-44.

In this Biblical story, four thousand people ate and were satisfied, with seven baskets of food left over, after seven loaves of bread and a few fish were distributed among them.

The miracle of the loaves teaches us that there are things which we can share, without losing them. A beautiful story, for instance. Or useful knowledge. They are, after all, food for the mind. Like the miraculous fish and loaves of bread, we can start with little, share them with others, feed thousands, and end up with more than we started with.

Everytime we share knowledge with the hungry, everytime we share a book or a tape with friends, we are, in a way, celebrating the miracle of the loaves.

2. A new offensive against the Third World

The most powerful countries of the world, led by the United States, are on the offensive again.

Unlike the colonial wars of old, or the Cold War to defend the "free world," they are raising this time a seemingly incongruous slogan for their new crusade: "protection of intellectual property rights."

At first glance, this U.S.-led protectionist campaign seems like a minor concern to both the Western and the Third World countries, an esoteric area that is only a side agenda among trade missions, business circles, and corporate lawyers.

In reality, intellectual property rights (IPR) are an emerging area of serious contention between developed and developing countries. A number of issues of growing importance are actually a reflection of this rising conflict.

Goodbye to low-cost textbooks

Thirty years ago, textbooks were so expensive that second-hand book shops flourished. Some of these shops can still be seen at the University Belt in Manila.

Ferdinand Marcos may have done a lot of bad things, but he did at least one good thing: he passed a decree permitting local publishers to reprint expensive foreign textbooks, to be sold on the local market only. Thus, he ushered an era of inexpensive

---

This paper was presented in a symposium held by the Third World Studies Center (TWSC) on May 30, 1993 in the University of the Philippines, Diliman campus.

textbooks. Many of our professionals and technicians here and abroad owe their education partly to this availability of low-cost books. To buy imported originals, we would have spent five to ten times the price of the local reprints.

Unfortunately, this era of affordable textbooks may soon be over. The U.S. now insists that we cannot go on "violating" their copyrights. It has threatened the Philippines with trade sanctions. Our government is afraid of losing its garments quota and other trade privileges with the U.S. So, to keep in the good graces of the U.S. government, our government has agreed to phase out the book reprinting law.

This means that local book reprints which have kept textbook costs relatively low will soon be banned, forcing us back to an era of expensive imported textbooks. With the cost of education going up, many poor students may soon find it too expensive to continue their education.

Welcome to the intellectual property rights (IPR) issue.

The U.S. is after much more than just an end to the reprinting of books. It is after a very strict implementation of copyrights. When you photocopy a chapter of a U.S. textbook, the U.S. says, "You are violating our copyrights. You must first ask for our permission, and you must pay us royalties for each photocopy." The U.S. won't allow us to reprint expensive textbooks; they may soon stop us from photocopying them too.

Affordable computing may soon end

Another area of school activity is becoming a center of IPR contention: computers. We all know how computer technology has become a very important area of knowledge and learning. Practically all schools now offer computer courses; there is even talk of making the teaching of computer technology mandatory. To use a computer means to use computer programs like DOS, Wordstar, Lotus, and Dbase. Right now, we need only twenty or maybe thirty pesos to buy a diskette copy. If we ask a friend, we can probably even get a copy for free.

Computer courses are now quite affordable because the cost of the reprinted manuals as well as of software copies are relatively low. Thus, all of us can aspire to acquire computer skills and improve our job opportunities in the process. However, this might also end soon. A school with twenty computers, the U.S. insists, should buy twenty original programs, at a hundred dollars or so per copy. If forced to do so, schools will simply pass on this additional cost to their students, once more raising the cost of education.

To make sure that we actually buy their software, the rental of computer programs may likewise be prohibited. One can rent a book or a video, both of which are copyrightable materials but they want to prohibit the rental of software, to close all avenues other than actually buying their hundred-dollar software.

Receiving license required?

The U.S. is also pressuring our government to require a license for satellite receivers, still another ramification of the IPR issue. The U.S. says that satellite transmissions are copyrighted and viewers must pay royalties to receive them. They insist that the government require licenses and charge fees for satellite receivers.

Is this wrong, some ask. After all, a rich satellite dish owner can presumably easily afford a license.

It is wrong because it sets a dangerous precedent. If one needs a license for satellite receivers, what about other receivers, like radio or TV sets? If the government gets away with satellite receiver licensing, it can cite exactly the same reasons to require licenses for television and radio receivers. And if it does so, then licenses for fax machines, video recorders, photocopying machines, and other means of sharing information could not be far behind.

To start controlling the movement of information and restricting citizen's rights to acquire and exchange information is to move in the direction of the police state. This is the dangerous direction set by the proposed licensing of satellite receivers. All for protecting the so-called intellectual property rights of the United States.

Clearly, IPRs are an emerging arena of conflict between developing and developed countries. Developing countries like us want – and need – easy and low-cost access to information. Developed countries – who own more than 90% of the IPRs in the world – want to restrict access only to those who are willing to pay the high prices that they charge.

Developing countries continue to appropriate information they need for themselves, a practice that is next to impossible to restrict because people willingly exchange information, like friends sharing diskettes, for instance. Developed countries, on the other hand, see this appropriation as a major loss of income for them. Thus they want "protection."

Copyrights, which involve "expressions" of ideas, like books, music, video tapes, and software, are a major IPR area. Patents are another. Here too, the contention between developed and developing countries is becoming more intense.

Developed countries are using patents more and more as a monopolistic device to prevent competition from developing countries, in the process preventing technological development of the latter from proceeding smoothly.

Higher pharmaceutical prices?

A major area of patent contention is the drug industry. In many countries, pharmaceutical products cannot be patented, because they are essential to maintain the people's health. In the Philippines, a drug – usually patented by a multinational company – receives full patent protection for only two years. Two years after a patented drug is introduced into the market, our government may authorize local firms to produce the drug locally and make it more affordable to people, in the same way reprinting makes books more affordable to students.

This is called compulsory licensing: the government issues a license to a local firm to produce a patented (or copyrighted) product, and compels the local producer to pay royalties to the original IPR owner. Compulsory licensing is an internationally-recognized mechanism to ensure access by Third World countries to new technologies and products. Many countries have, in fact, used this mechanism in pharmaceuticals, food products, and agricultural implements.

Now, the U.S. wants the government to abolish compulsory licensing. Already, the Lina bill on intellectual and industrial property is pending in the Senate, with any mention of compulsory licensing in its provisions deleted.

Privatizing life forms

Another big issue in IPR is the privatization of life forms through breeders' rights and patents. This issue includes: (for details, see Part II)

- control over plant varieties and seeds through plant breeders' rights,
- the collection of traditional varieties in advanced countries and their disappearance from farmers' fields due to monoculture,
- ownership of whole classes of biological materials and processes through patents on life forms,
- the Human Genome Project, and the patenting of human genetic sequences,
- the Human Genome Diversity Project, which is gathering genetic material of indigenous and tribal peoples worldwide to be preserved for future commercial exploitation.

This is the natural consequence of extending IPR to life forms: the reduction of God's creations – plants, animals and human life – into commercial possibilities that corporations must compete for and establish monopoly ownership over.

What have all these examples of the IPR offensive got to do with economic development?

IPRs such as copyrights and patents are actually a grant by the State of a monopoly over the use of ideas and expressions of ideas. In short, they are monopolies over information. Patents and copyrights are currently the main form of owning information, and they also happen to be highly monopolistic in nature.

IPRs have become such an important issue for the U.S. and other advanced countries because they have become information economies, and have to establish firmly their ownership – in fact, their monopoly – over information. Their demand for the "protection of intellectual property rights" is in reality a major campaign to firmly establish and consolidate their monopoly over information goods. This is why U.S. diplomats and negotiators, whenever they open their mouths, will never fail to mention the protection of intellectual property rights in their agenda. They inserted it in the proposed Military Bases Agreement, which, thankfully, our Senate rejected. They included it in the North American Free Trade Agreement (NAFTA). Every time they talk to a Third World country, a small one like Malaysia or a huge one like China, their overriding demand is always IPR protection.

In the negotiations at the Uruguay Round of the General Agreement on Trade and Tariffs (GATT), for instance, Western countries have introduced a new theme, which they call "trade-related" intellectual property rights or TRIPs. GATT is a multilateral negotiating forum that is supposedly meant to reduce tariff and non-tariff barriers to trade. While monopolies have previously been considered barriers to free trade, the TRIPs proposal has turned the idea around. It has glossed over the monopolistic nature of patents and copyrights by calling them "trade-related." The proposal now claims that patent and copyright infringements are "distortions of trade flows," which are therefore subject to GATT action. Because GATT has well-developed mechanisms for retaliatory action, adoption by GATT of the TRIPS proposal by Western countries will be a major setback in Third World efforts towards facilitating technology transfer.

Our government does not seem to realize this. Instead of fighting for access to technology to hasten our own development, we are surrendering to U.S. demands that will serve to stunt the development of our own information sector.

We are thus giving the U.S., on a silver platter, whole new monopolies over information.

Curiously, we hear very little protest from affected sectors on this issue. Many are simply completely unaware of the issue. Recently, President Fidel Ramos formed a presidential committee to study this issue, and the "NGO" representative comes from COMPACT, the industry association that represents the interests of U.S. companies in the Philippines!

Furthermore, the U.S. and our government have managed to keep the IPR negotiations in a low profile by subsuming them under trade negotiations or some others talks where the Philippines appears to be receiving trade favors from the U.S. government. In actuality, the U.S. is wangling huge concessions from the Philippine government on this issue, at the expense of our educational system, health system, science and technology development, and the indigenous peoples.

The only way to prevent this hemorrhage of concessions is to build a strong popular movement to counterbalance U.S. threats and pressures against our government. The people's minimum demands with respect to this issue should include the following:

1. Appoint genuine NGO representatives in the presidential committee on intellectual property rights issues.

2. Retain the book reprinting law.
3. Retain the compulsory licensing of pharmaceutical products.
4. Strengthen compulsory licensing and expand its coverage to software and other items deemed essential by the government.
5. Do not allow the patenting of life forms.

We must ask the government to act on these demands now, before it completely succumbs to U.S. pressure and brings about a new era of colonialism.

3. U.S. piracy in the 19th century

Nineteenth century America was a major center of piracy. The principal target of U.S. pirates was the rich variety of British books and periodicals. The U.S. was a perennial headache among British authors and publishers, because foreign authors had no rights in America. American publishers and printers, led by Harpers of New York and Careys of Philadelphia, routinely violated British copyright and "reprinted a very wide range of British publications."

James Barnes, who wrote an excellent book on this subject, said that the Americans were "suspicious about international copyright," and were afraid that recognizing international copyright meant "exploitation and domination of their book trade." Barnes noted that "as a young nation, the United States wanted the freedom to borrow literature as well as technology from any quarter of the globe, and it was not until 1891 that Congress finally recognized America's literary independence by authorizing reciprocal copyright agreements with foreign powers."

Throughout the 19th century, Barnes writes, a group of American authors and Anglophiles led a persistent but futile campaign to get a copyright treaty between the U.S. and Britain ratified, but their efforts were overcome by a much stronger lobby for free access to British publications. But time and again, the U.S. Senate rejected proposed laws or treaties that would have granted copyright to foreign authors in the United States.

This chapter is based principally on the excellent book Authors, Publishers and Politicians *by James J. Barnes. John Tebbel's somewhat biased account in* A History of Book Publishing in the United States *also details the futile attempts in the 1870's and 1880's to pass U.S. legislation that would protect the rights of foreign authors, and the developments that led to the eventual adoption of the 1891 U.S. Copyright Act which extended some protection to foreign authors.*

As Barnes put it, "If Americans thought of the topic [i.e., copyright] at all they were concerned with protecting domestic copyright and not the rights of foreigners. As a country, nineteenth-century America was akin to a present-day underdeveloped nation which recognizes its dependence on those more commercially and technologically advanced, and desires the fruits of civilization in the cheapest and most convenient ways. Reprinting English literature seemed easy and inexpensive, and so America borrowed voraciously."

Barnes continued: "In 1831, 'An Act to Amend the Several Acts Respecting Copyrights' was signed. It extended the copyright term from fourteen to twenty-eight years, with the option of renewal for an additional fourteen. If an author died, his widow or children could apply for the extension. For the first time, the law allowed musical compositions to be copyrighted. But not a word on international copyright. In fact, foreign authors were explicitly barred from protection, which in essence safeguarded reprints."

Even the U.S. president at that time, John Quincy Adams, was himself "strongly opposed to international copyright."

In 1837, Senator Henry Clay introduced a copyright bill before the U.S. Senate. Within days, "a flood of negative memorials reached Washington," and objections deluged both houses of Congress. The U.S. Senate's Patent Committee rejected "the intention of the measure," its reasons sounding very much like the justification today of Third World countries for their liberal attitude towards intellectual property. The Committee's reasons were:

- "A copyright agreement would promote higher book prices and smaller editions. The point was driven home by comparing the retail prices of new books in England and America, for it was universally acknowledged that English books were disproportionately more expensive."
- "A large portion of the U.S. publishers' business "would be reduced perhaps as much as nine-tenths, certainly as

much as three-fourths, if copyright be granted to foreign books."

- "Many more English authors stood to gain by such a treaty because American authors rarely if ever received favourable publishing terms in Britain."
- Copyright has never been regarded among nations as "property standing on the footing of wares or merchandise, or as a proper subject for national protection against foreign spoilation." Every government has always been left to make such regulations as it thinks proper, "with no right of complaint or interference by any other government."
- British authors only want the U.S. Congress to pass an act which will enable them to "monopolize the publication here [in the U.S.] as well as in England, of all English works for the supply of the American market."

The Committee also explained why international patents were acceptable but not international copyright: "American ingenuity in the arts and practical sciences, would derive at least as much benefit from international patent laws, as that of foreigners. Not so with authorship and book-making. The difference is too obvious to admit of controversy."

In short, the Americans stood to gain a lot of benefits by recognizing international patents; and they likewise stood to gain a lot of benefits by not recognizing international copyright. It was purely a matter of national interest.

The U.S. printers advanced their own arguments for reprinting British publications without regard for international copyright:

- They were making available to the American people cheap books which would otherwise be very costly if they had to compensate foreign authors. It was generally acknowledged that the low prices of American books would inevitably rise after the passage of a copyright treaty.

- Access by the American printing industry to British works provided Americans with thousands of jobs.
- British authors and publishers would exercise "complete control over the publication of their works in the U.S." Popular British writers "could then exact their own prices for their books when sold here [in the U.S.]" Thus copyright would not only enhance the profits of major authors, but at the same time protect and encourage second-rate foreign talent.
- International copyright "would also interfere with the laws of supply and demand because it encouraged monopoly which was never in the public interest."
- Tariff duties might be appropriate for some industries, but they were never intended to confer a monopoly on a producer.
- Books are "unlike other commodities"; whereas it took the same amount of labor to create each new hat or boot, "the multiplication of copies of a book meant a saving on each additional facsimile."
- Authors and publishers enjoy copyright "only by virtue of statute law;" copyright is not "absolute and natural ownership." The right of individual property is subordinate to the public good which is "best served through free competition and cheap reprints."

Several bills were introduced in 1870, 1871 and again in 1872, but they were all opposed by American publishers and the printing unions, because they would "make English books more expensive, really benefit American authors as a class, and permanently injure the interests of book manufacturers."

And so it went. In the early 1880's, the copyright movement gained more strength, but not quite enough to overcome the more powerful forces that benefitted from free and unrestricted access to foreign publications.

By this time, however, the U.S. had already accumulated a wealth of American-authored works which were themselves widely reprinted abroad. American books like *Uncle Tom's Cabin* became quite popular in England. Also, U.S. authors and their publishers had acquired considerable political clout. The U.S. was ready to "protect" foreign authors, so that it could in turn demand protection for American authors abroad.

In July 1891, the U.S. Congress adopted the Chace International Copyright Act of 1891, establishing a framework for bilateral copyright agreements based on reciprocity. While the act granted copyright to resident and nonresident authors for a period of 28 years, renewable for another 14, it also set very difficult conditions, reflecting the interests of the U.S. publishing industry:

- A foreign book had to be published in the U.S. not later than its publication in its home country.
- All manufacturing of books, photos, chromos and lithographs had to be done in the U.S. (This is the so-called "manufacturing clause," which is today protested by the U.S., when Third World governments adopt it to ensure that a technology is actually worked in their own country.)
- Foreign copyrighted books in English, photographs, chromos, lithographs or plates could be imported for sale, but not more than two copies at a time could be imported for use, and these were subject to duty.
- Foreign works published before July 1, 1891 may not be copyrighted.

In 1952, the U.S. joined the Universal Copyright Convention (UCC), but not the Berne Convention, which was considered the "premier instrument of international copyright." Under the UCC, the U.S. retained such protectionist measures as the requirement of manufacture in the United States.

In the meantime, the U.S. had been exerting tremendous pressures on Third World governments to adopt strict intellectual property laws and to strengthen their enforcement. By the late 1980's, a number of governments, including Singapore, Hong Kong, Taiwan and South Korea in Asia, had finally succumbed to U.S. pressure.

And so in 1989, the U.S. finally and belatedly acceded to the Berne copyright convention.

4. The "piracy" of intellectuals

Computers need computer programs to run them. In recent years, computers have become more affordable. As a result, a local market for copies of computer programs is thriving.

Many Filipino computer users copy the programs they need from computer shops, or from a number of computer bulletin board systems which have proliferated around the metropolis. They then give copies of these programs to friends and colleagues, who, in turn, give copies to other friends and colleagues.

In the words of Western software companies, they are pirates. To copy commercial software and give it away to friends and colleagues is called piracy.

We've seen pirates in movies and they're a mean bunch. They are villains who steal, kill, and plunder. At the movie's ending, when these scoundrels get their just due, the audience invariably applauds. It is no fun to be called a pirate. Or to be treated like one.

Filipinos who exchange software and share them with others freely hardly resemble the pirates in the movies. Yet, according to Western software firms, copying without paying is piracy. So, we are pirates just the same. And we're no better than those one-eyed villains who kill and plunder for a living.

We've seen people who come from or work for Western software firms. Well groomed, in business coat and tie, they look the antithesis of the pirate they hate so much. They come and visit

---

A version of this article appeared in the Third World Resurgence, *January-February, 1993 (No. 29-30: pp. 57-58). TWR is published by the Third World Network, an international network of non-government organizations and individuals working on development issues.*

this country of pirates, and perhaps make a little study how much they are losing from piracy in the Philippines.

Quite a number of them, however, come to the country to do some pirating themselves.

But they don't pirate software, which is apparently beyond their dignity. They pirate people. They pirate those who write the software. They pirate our best systems analysts, our best engineers, our best programmers, and our best computer operators.

The advanced countries of the West routinely pirate from the Third World our best professionals and skilled workers, but begrudge us peoples of the Third World if we engage in some piracy ourselves. They accuse the Third World of "piracy of intellectual property," yet they themselves engage in the "piracy of intellectuals."

In truth, there is quite a difference between pirating intellectual property and pirating intellectuals.

For example, it costs our country perhaps ten thousand dollars to train one doctor. Training a second doctor would cost another ten thousand dollars. Training ten doctors would cost a hundred thousand dollars. In short, given an 'original' doctor, it would cost us as much to make each 'copy' of the original. When the Americans pirate our doctors, they take away an irreplaceable resource, for it takes more than ten years to train a new doctor. The Philippines has approximately one doctor for every 6,700 citizens. When the U.S. pirates this doctor, it denies 6,700 Filipinos of the services of a doctor. And every year, the U.S. takes away hundreds of our doctors. How many Filipinos died because they could not get the services of a doctor on time?

What about a computer program? Whatever amount Lotus Corporation spent in developing their spreadsheet program, it costs practically nothing to make a second or third copy of the program. It would take a few seconds for them to make each copy. When we Filipinos pirate their program, we have not stolen any irreplaceable resource, nor will it take Lotus 10 years to replace the program, nor have we denied any American citizen the use of the spreadsheet program. It is still there, for Americans to use. We make a copy of their program, we don't steal it, because we have not taken anything away. We have made our own copy, but they still have the original.

Pirating a computer program is quite different from pirating a doctor. When the U.S. pirates our doctors, it doesn't take a copy and leave the original behind. Instead, it takes the original and leaves nothing behind.

But you can't compare the two, some would say. The U.S. pays for our doctors with much higher salaries, so you can't call it piracy. Third World countries copy software without paying the commercial price, therefore they are pirates. If you have the money to pirate people, it stops being called piracy and becomes a respectable activity. But if you can't afford it, sorry.

On the other hand, we can also say that when the West draws away our professionals with attractive salary offers, they take away not a 'copy' but the 'original,' and we are left with none. We've lost the services of these professionals for good. If we make a copy of their software, we never take away the original, and we leave them with as much as they originally had. We can even gift them an extra copy, gratis. To call this stealing is to speak in metaphors; as in a stolen glance, or a stolen kiss. They might say they lost a sale, but it is only an opportunity to sell and make a profit that they are referring to. In many instances, the opportunity isn't even there at all.

It is as if a company who insists on a monopoly of fish, accused us of causing them lost sales because we let loose fingerlings all over the lakes and rivers, so that people may catch them and eat. Fish, like software, love to go forth and multiply, whatever else their original creators might have intended. And it is all for the better, because this means more people can enjoy them.

In fact, this distinction sets the new information technologies apart from the traditional services sector. Information, if it already exists in the modern high- technology form such as computer files on a diskette, can be duplicated at practically no cost. It is therefore in perfect form to be given away freely to those who need it. Given a computer, software would in effect reproduce itself on the machine at the slightest provocation, copying itself for next to nothing. However, there is, so far, no easy way to freely duplicate the accumulated information in a doctor's head. So we must spend ten thousand dollars and more than ten years, just to make a second copy.

This is why we actually do very little damage when we 'pirate' a copy of a computer program, and why the U.S. does a lot of harm when it pirates one of our doctors.

This piracy debate will become even more important in the future because advanced countries are now developing computer programs that can mimic what goes on in a doctor's mind. The United States, which has been routinely pirating our best doctors and nurses for decades, will probably raise a big howl if we pirated this one program, even if we had no intention of denying them the original.

Copying software is a benign case of piracy. Pirating doctors is a malignant case.

We have been long-time victims of this malignant case of piracy by Western countries. They should be the last to complain when they are affected with a benign one.

5. GATT: Free Trade or Monopoly Growth?

Everybody knows that the opposite of free trade is monopoly. Monopolies tend to restrict free trade; free trade tends to break down monopolies. By breaking down monopolies and other barriers to trade, the General Agreement on Tariffs and Trade (GATT) is supposed to lead to free trade between nations.

Curiously enough, however, a major section of GATT – some say it is the centerpiece – is unabashedly pro-monopoly, strengthening the scope of monopolies and making it more difficult to break them.

Patents and copyrights are monopolies

These monopolies are the statutory monopolies granted to authors and inventors which give them exclusive rights to enjoy, make, copy and sell their works. These monopolies are called copyrights in the case of authors, and patents in the case of inventors. Collectively, they are known under GATT as intellectual property rights (IPR). They protect ownership over what might be called "information goods."

Historically, these monopolies were not a natural right, but a special privilege granted by the State, in order to reward intellectuals for their creative contributions to society's storehouse of knowledge, or to encourage inventors to disclose the secrets of their inventions rather than carry them to their graves. Such monopolies were usually granted for a limited period only: up to

---

This paper was circulated by the author in 1994, when the decision to join GATT was being debated in the Philippine Senate, in the media and among the public.

several decades after an author's death, in recognition of the possibility that his work may become commercially successful only posthumously; fourteen years for an invention, which was equal to twice the traditional apprenticeship period of a craftsman.

Governments also made sure that such monopolies would not be abused. As noted above, the life of the monopoly was usually limited. In addition, the State usually reserved the right, if it was deemed in the national interest, to authorize others to commercialize a copyrighted or patented work.

Restricting monopolies

In the case of patents, a common government requirement is the "working" of the patent. That is, the patent holder must actually manufacture the patented product and make it available to the population in sufficient quantities.

The most common mechanism for the government to provide others access to a protected (i.e., patented or copyrighted) work is the compulsory license. Normally, a third party who wants to commercialize a protected work must ask for a license from the patent/copyright holder. The latter may grant a license, in exchange for some payment, or may refuse the request. Under compulsory licensing, the third party approaches not the patent or copyright holder, but the government. It is the government which issues to the third party a license to commercialize a protected product; at the same time, the government also normally compels the third party to pay royalties (typically 2-5%) to the patent or copyright holder.

International agreements recognize compulsory licensing as a valid option, especially for developing countries, for accessing technologies at lower cost.

Thus, the Philippines had its Book Reprinting Law, which for years provided our students and professionals access to relatively low-cost textbooks and manuals.

In many countries, pharmaceutical and food products were considered vital to the national interest. So, they were either excluded from the patent system altogether, or were subject to compulsory licensing within a few years after they were introduced into the market.

In general, therefore, a country's intellectual property rights laws reflect a delicate balance between the interests of authors and inventors, on one hand, and the interests of the rest of society, on the other hand.

GATT strengthens monopolies

Under GATT, this delicate balance is being tilted heavily in favor of monopolies. This pro-monopoly trend can be seen in the following GATT features:

- compulsory licensing has been severely restricted
- copyright holders have been extended rental rights
- patent holders have been extended importation rights
- in infringement cases, the burden of proof is on the accused, not the accuser
- secrets are now protected without need for "disclosure"
- patent and copyright enforcement has been strengthened

Restricted compulsory licensing

This mechanism has been rendered much less effective. Before, the only major requirement was an actual capability to commercialize a product. Under GATT, a whole new set of restrictive requirements has been adopted. A patented product, for instance, may only be subjected to compulsory licensing under the these conditions:

- the compulsory license applicant must first try to get authorization from the patent holder on reasonable commercial terms and conditions;

- the applicant must persist in his efforts for a reasonable period of time;
- the license must be terminated as soon as the circumstances which led to it cease to exist and are unlikely to recur;
- the patent holder should receive adequate payment, based on economic value; and
- such licenses are subject to judicial or other independent review.

Under these conditions, it becomes much easier now for patent holders to frustrate applications for a compulsory license and preserve their monopolies.

Rental rights

For computer programs, cinematographic works, and – optionally – other copyrighted works, GATT wants countries to grant holders the right to permit or prohibit third parties from renting out the copyrighted works. The text says: "a [GATT] Member shall provide authors and their successors in title the right to authorize or to prohibit the commercial rental to the public of originals or copies of their copyright works."

For instance, many consumers find it too expensive to buy their own copies of video programs or laser disc programs. The low-cost option for them would be to rent such programs from a video shop. But a foreign motion picture company may decide to sell tapes of its movies locally, and prohibit the rentals of the same tapes, so that those who want to see the tape will have no choice but to buy an original copy.

Importation rights

For a patented product, the holder is granted the right "to prevent third parties not having the owner's consent from the acts of: making, using, offering for sale, selling, or importing" the product. For a patented process, the holder is granted the right "to prevent third parties not having the owners' consent from the act of using the process, and from the acts of: using, offering for sale, selling or importing" products obtained directly from that process.

In the past, countries were insistent that a patent be "worked" (i.e., manufactured) in their country in order to facilitate the transfer of technology to the local population. With the introduction of importation rights, the holder would not anymore be obligated to "work" a patent in a particular country. This would make the technology involved in the manufacture of the product less accessible to a country.

Suppose, also, a multinational company sells a pharmaceutical product in the Philippines at prices which we consider exhorbitant. A third party discovers that the same product is sold in Hong Kong by the same company at half the price. Should the third party import the product from Hong Kong for sale in the Philippines, the multinational can prohibit this importation, leaving local consumers no alternative source for the product. This is monopoly, pure and simple.

Guilty until proven innocent

For patented processes, the burden of proof lies with the alleged infringer of the patent and not the accuser.

This is the text of the relevant GATT provision: "if the subject matter of a patent is a process for obtaining a product, the judicial authorities shall have the authority to order the defendant to prove that the process to obtain an identical product is different from the patented process....any identical product when produced without the consent of the patent owner shall, in the absence of proof to the contrary, be deemed to have been obtained by the patented process."

No need to disclose

The patent extended the inventor a limited monopoly in exchange for his disclosure of the "secrets" of his invention. Thus, inventors were required to provide complete working drawings and other details of their patented work, so that anybody skilled in the state-of-the-art would be able to reproduce the invention. This was society's way of ensuring that society may eventually benefit from a protected work.

GATT goes further and now provides for the protection of undisclosed information. By protecting information without requiring its disclosure for future use by the rest of society, GATT again manifests its pro-monopoly bias, in total disregard of the original intent of intellectual property rights protection.

Stronger enforcement

GATT now dictates the details of enforcement rules and practices that countries must adopt to ensure that IPRs are effectively protected. If it was possible before for countries to give lip service to IPR protection while holding off enforcement, this would be much more difficult to do under a GATT regime, as the rights of holders and the obligations of law enforcers and the judicial system are spelled out in great detail.

Protectionism is anathema to GATT. Yet, the agreement is protectionist in favor of IPRs. Monopolies are anathema to free trade. Yet, GATT is strengthening information monopolies through TRIPS.

GATT's bias in favor of the interests of developed economics seems clear enough.

6. IPR: a clash of value-systems

Over the past twelve years or so, I have been working with computers practically on a daily basis. And when one works with computers – especially with computer software and data – one is working with practically pure information. In the past few years, I've been studying social issues relating to information technology and exploring the possibility that information technologies can be used for democratization and popular empowerment.

In the course of my work with computers, I've gained a few insights about the nature of information.

We know, for instance, that information is not matter; it has no mass and it doesn't occupy physical space. It is intangible. Scientists define information in relation to the concept of uncertainty: information is that which resolves or reduces uncertainty.

What is interesting is that since information is non-material, it is very easy to reproduce. As soon as you share information with somebody else, you reproduce it. Talking before you right now reproduces information many-fold. Broadcasting information over radio or TV can reproduce information thousands – even millions – of times over. Every time I copy a diskette, this quality of information manifests itself. Whether it is a conversation, a public performance, an electronic broadcast, or the copying of tapes and diskettes, it is clear that once information is generated, the cost of reproducing it eventually becomes negligible.

This paper was presented at the 11th Annual Conference of the Philippine International Forum (PIF), held on February 22-24, 1994, in Cebu City. PIF is an organization of expatriates, many of them church-related, working with Philippine non-government organizations.

Let me present it differently. When I let a friend copy a computer program, I do not lose possession of the program. I still have my own copy. Sharing one's worldly belongings is difficult for many to do because to give away material goods is to lose possession of these goods. But sharing knowledge and information is the most natural thing to do, because we don't lose them when we share them.

Thus, sharing information freely comes naturally. It is most natural for computer users to share programs among themselves. How can one be so selfish as to deny a friend a copy of a program if one won't lose the program by sharing it?

However, now comes the Business Software Association (BSA) and the government of the United States, asserting that copying computer programs is stealing, that for every copy we share, we are actually "stealing" hundreds of dollars from American corporations. This is quite a clash of values, isn't it?

The first major observation that came out of my twelve years of work with computers and information technology is that it takes very little to share information, and people share information freely.

This is true of knowledge and information we hold in our minds. It is true of music, poems, and songs. It is true of computer programs and computer data. It is also true of genetic information as contained in seeds, plants and animals.

But this problem with the BSA and the U.S. government remains: they want to stop us from sharing freely. Instead, they want us to acknowledge the ownership claims that some have staked on information. These ownership claims are in the form of exclusive usage and copying rights, or intellectual property rights (IPR) – their intellectual property rights.

Piracy: good or bad?

It is clearly to our interest to dip freely into the world's storehouse of knowledge and adopt technologies which might be useful for our development. When it was still a developing country in the 18th and 19th centuries, the U.S. was one of the worst pirates of British books and publications. When it was trying to catch up with the U.S. and Europe, Japan also freely copied Western technologies. Taiwan did the same. So did Korea.

When the U.S. sent spy satellites in space, countries complained that the U.S. was taking away strategic information and violating their sovereign control over their own territories. The U.S. insisted that it was free get this information whenever it wanted, even to sell them back to those countries, if they were willing to pay for them. U.S. commercial satellites then started beaming video programming into other countries. When those whose culture considered the video content objectionable complained, the U.S. invoked the concept of "free flow of information" to insist that it had the right to beam these programs. Yet, when local people who developed a taste for U.S. programs taped these satellite broadcasts and distributed them locally, the U.S. started complaining why people were receiving and copying their broadcasts without paying for them. According to their twisted logic, this was a violation of their IPRs.

The U.S. sends its people worldwide to interview local healers and acquire their centuries-old healing knowledge, which had been passed from generation to generation. When we copy U.S. books to acquire their knowledge, we are accused of piracy. U.S. scientists freely take away all kinds of microorganisms, plants and other sources of medicinal substances from us. Yet, when we copy the drugs that have been developed from these substances, we are also accused of piracy.

In short, information acquisition has been defined so that when it is bad for the interests of the U.S. and other advanced countries but good for us, it is called "piracy" and "free-riding," but when information acquisition is good for their interests and bad for us, it falls under labels like "free flow of information" and "common heritage of mankind."

For those who still think the U.S. value system is more "natural," let me tell you another story. This one comes from the Bible:

> When it was evening, his disciples came to him and said, "We are in a lonely place and it is now late. You should send these people away so they can go to the villages and buy something for themselves to eat."
>
> But Jesus replied, "They do not need to go away; you give them something to eat." They answered, "We have nothing here but five loaves and two fishes." Jesus said to them, "Bring them here to me."
>
> Then he had everyone sit down on the grass. He took the five loaves and the two fishes, raised his eyes to heaven, pronounced the blessing, broke the loaves and handed them to the disciples to distribute to the people. And they all ate, and everyone had enough; then the disciples gathered up the leftovers, filling twelve baskets.

The message behind the act of sharing miraculous loaves of bread must be extremely important indeed, because the miracle occurs twice in Biblical passages. My Muslim and Buddhist friends have told me about similar stories in their own cultures, like the story of the miraculous dates and milk, or of the jar that was a bottomless source of water. How significant, that the world's greatest religions would teach the same lesson through analogous parables.

Indeed, how can you be selfish, if you can give things away and have more than what you started with? How can we deny a good from friends, if we can also keep it for ourselves?

Given the issue of intellectual property rights, the first major question crops up: why is it, that some societies extol information sharing, while other societies stake monopolistic ownership claims on information goods? Why do rural folk exchange seeds freely, while corporations want monopoly rights over seeds through patents? Why do BSA and the U.S. government want to impose – as they've successfully done through the General Agreement on Trade and Tariffs (GATT) – their value-systems concerning information over our own value-systems?

This took me to the U.S. economy. There must be something in the U.S. economy which was propelling the extension of highly monopolistic private property concepts to areas like information and life forms. The most important observation that emerged from my readings was this: the U.S. economy had undergone a fundamental change in the nature of the goods that it produces. A few decades back, U.S. products were industrial goods of the tangible, material kind – cars, television sets, and machineries, for example. U.S. products today are fundamentally different; they contain intangible, non-material goods – books, software, video and audio tapes, databases. The storage medium may make them seem tangible, but much of their prices reflect the intangible content, protected through patents or copyrights.

It is this fundamental shift in the nature of U.S. products which has led to the emergence of a highly monopolistic ownership system over information goods. Let me go back to my first observation: it takes very little to copy information. We know, for example, how little it costs to copy a diskette. The corollary observation, however, is that if one can prevent others from freely copying information, such as those sold in diskettes or tapes, then they will have market value, and because the reproduction cost is minimal, the margins of profit would be extremely high indeed. It is the high profit margins derived from the sale of monopolistically-owned information products which led to the rapid growth of the U.S. information sector. With the growth of this sector, particularly because it controlled the media, came the increasing dominance of the value-system that supports monopolistic private ownership systems over information.

This is the fundamental difference between an industrial economy, as the U.S. economy was several decades ago, and an information economy, as the U.S. economy is today: an industrial economy produces tangible, material goods while an information economy produces intangible, non-material goods. Material goods require raw materials which are then transformed into finished products by human labor. Information goods are mostly the result of mental work and, once created, may be reproduced at practically no cost. They may also be shared without loss.

Having made this comparison, I went further and analyzed an agricultural economy, likewise from the viewpoint of the nature of the goods produced. Here, I came to a somewhat different conclusion from what has traditionally been considered agricultural work. Traditionally, agricultural and industrial sectors were differentiated on the basis of land. Simplistically put, working the land was considered agricultural work; working with factory machines to make finished products from raw materials was considered industrial work.

I realized that on the basis of the nature of the goods that they produce, a clearer and much more insightful dividing line existed between the agriculture and the industrial sectors, just as clear and insightful as the material/non-material divide between the industrial and the information sectors. What is this dividing line?

This is the line between the living and the non-living.

In agriculture we find issues of birth, growth, reproduction and death. Here we grapple with the relation of human beings with nature and the rest of the living world. While the industrial sector involves the physical transformation of dead matter into finished products through the application of human labor, the agriculture sector involves the regeneration and the reproduction of life through the operation of natural processes. What a world of difference!

Consider driving a nail into wood: to drive nail into the wood, one must hit it with a hammer. One must apply human or machine power on dead matter to transform it into a finished product. Consider the typical industrial operations: punching, drilling, boring, milling, grinding, melting, etc. Imagine the kind of value-system or – to use another term – world-view, that will emerge when this is one's activity eight or more hours a day, most days of the week.

Consider, on the other hand, raising a crop. You water the plants; you give them tender loving care. You cannot even speed up the process. As the song goes, there is a time for everything under heaven. This is an entirely different value-system we are talking about. You can perhaps understand why I myself prefer to call the agriculture sector the ecology sector.

Finally, in a roundabout way, I have come to the gist of my presentation.

Based on the nature of the goods and services they produce, economies have three major production sectors: the agriculture sector, the industrial sector and the information sector. In countries like the Philippines, the agriculture sector remains the dominant sector. In the newly industrialized countries (NICs), the industrial sector has become dominant. In the U.S. and to a lesser extent Europe, it is the information sector which is now becoming dominant.

With each sector can be associated a set of value-systems or world-views.

Agriculture

The agriculture or ecology sector promotes a world-view that reflects our relationship with nature and the processes of regeneration and reproduction of life. Whether one is living off nature as a hunter/gatherer, planting food crops, domesticating animals for their milk and meat, or raising a family, we have to come to terms with the great laws of nature; we have to fit ourselves into the pace and tempo of nature's own processes. We must learn to adapt, to live in harmony with our surroundings. It is in agricultural activities where we are in the best position to appreciate that we are part of nature and are nurtured by it, with an obligation to nurture it in turn.

My wife comes from a farming family. Her first instinctive action, after eating a delicious fruit, is to save its seeds. My grandmother used to save everything she could: pieces of thread, pieces of paper, pieces of wood, pieces of metal. She knew they would be of use someday. She was expressing an ecological principle: in nature, nothing is wasted. In most rural communities, frugality remains a virtue – a lesson picked up from centuries of indigenous ecological learning.

It is in the ecology sector where spirituality easily takes root, because there is so much in nature and life processes that proceed without human intervention and are beyond our means to control and even, perhaps, to understand.

Industry

The industrial sector, on the other hand, expresses a world-view that reflects the central role of human labor power in transforming dead matter into a finished product. In nature, living things grow even without human intervention. But dead matter cannot transform itself into a finished product. Human labor power, frequently magnified by machines and technology, must be applied on the raw material, to mould and transform it into a product. We can see here the central role of power in material transformation. The history of technology might be seen as the development of various ways by which power can be brought to bear upon dead matter to transform it into a useful product. In our local language, to be compared to a nail means to move only after a shove. The shepherd and the crop grower, who have no choice but to bide their time and keep in step with nature's own tempo, must appear slothful indeed to workers and industrialists who transform raw materials by their own labor or by the power of machines.

The difference between material and non-material goods is qualitative. Put five pieces of bread (of the non-miraculous variety) on the table and tell ten hungry men to get one piece each and one can expect keen competition for possession of the pieces. They have a term for this in mathematics: zero-sum games. These are situations where the gain of one means somebody else's loss. In order to win, you must defeat somebody else. A piece of bread in their hands means one less for me. So, I must fight for my piece. International balance of trade is another example of a zero-sum game. For a country to attain a positive balance of trade, some of its partners must show a negative balance of trade, because by definition, the sum total of all exports and imports of all countries is zero. This is true with material goods that are scarce, which is almost always the case because we can never have an infinite supply of material goods. Zero-sum games are, by nature, highly competitive games. Socialist economies underestimated this aspect of competition for material goods, which emanates from the very nature of material goods. It was their pitfall.

The information sector

On the other hand, the acquisition of information is not a zero-sum game. If I put a diskette on the table and told everybody to make a copy for themselves, I can still keep my copy afterwards. Your gain is not my loss. If everyone put their diskettes on the table for others to copy, we will all have gained in the process. This is what mathematicians call a positive-sum game. Positive-sum games are highly cooperative. If socialist advocates erred in thinking they could abolish competition for material goods, they stand on much more solid ground in advocating socialist principles for information. By their very nature, information goods are public goods and the urge to share is completely in harmony with the nature of information.

However, work in the information sector can also develop a sense of omnipotence and absolute power that can distort the sense of the information creator. Those who have done some computer programming, or even played a simple video game, will know exactly what I mean. Because information is non-material and intangible, it does not need the kind of raw materials and energy supply that naturally puts a "limit to growth" on material goods production. The concept of the infinite (both in growth and in power) comes closer to reality in the information sector. One can create something out of nothing, create virtual worlds where one can become a virtual god. One can wield unlimited power and be in total control of "reality." Because the information sector has only recently become a major sector, it is hard to fully comprehend the implications of such illusions of absolute power and total control. These concepts of power and control emerged strongly in industrial economies, but they may reach their full expression in information economies.

Misapplied values

A very common problem with value-systems is the misapplication of value-systems (or world-views) which might be appropriate for one sector of the economy but not for another sector. This has happened most often with the industrial sector's value system, which may be called industrialism. Industrialism puts the power of human actions (amplified by machines) at the center of the universe. Nothing will get done if you don't roll up your sleeves to do it. Put in more inputs and more power and you will get more outputs. Put in more workers and money and you will get it done faster. This attitude becomes the dominant attitude not only in the production of material goods but also in social relations and in politics.

Coupled with profit-motivated commodity production, this view has led to a concept of growth without limit, of production for the market, of market expansion. True, this has led to the availability of a vast variety of goods for popular convenience and comfort. But it has also led to the profligate use of raw materials and energy sources from nature. It has led to inhuman monstrosities, both of the capitalist and the socialist kind, and to environmental disasters, some of which threaten the very existence of life on earth. It has led to the mindless production of commodities whose main purpose is not to satisfy genuine human needs but to generate profits. It has led to the emergence of junk culture, whose main purpose is to create demand for commodities and raise profit levels, which will in turn pay for the creation of more junk culture – a cancerous growth of decadence, commodity production and profit accumulation.

The concept of private property, while it emerges naturally from the zero-sum nature of material goods acquisition, has expanded way beyond the range of dead matter and material goods. It has grown more absolute. A very monopolistic expression may be found in the concept of intellectual property rights, another misapplication of the private property concepts of industrialism. Under this concept, information may not only be privatized but also opened for monopoly claims of ownership. This concept was first innocuously applied to literary works and inventions, but has since expanded to cover a vast range of knowledge and information goods. Now it even includes genetic information and processes in microorganisms, plants, animals, and, yes, human beings. It is curious to note that the claimant to intellectual property rights thinks of information as a landlord thinks of land: once you successfully stake a claim of ownership over a piece of it, you can sit down and charge the rest of society rents for the use of your property.

Briefly, these are the different value-systems that emerge from the three sectors:

1. The ecology sector teaches us appreciation and respect for life and the need for harmony with nature and its processes. On the other hand, it develops a somewhat passive attitude towards life and the environment.

2. The industrial sector teaches us the value of work and the capacity of people to transform their surroundings. On the other hand, this can result in overaggressiveness and excessive competition.

3. The information sector teaches us the value of cooperation and of sharing knowledge freely. On the other hand, because the intellectual creator feels a sense of total control and absolute power, it can lead to a very distorted sense of reality.

Which value-system should we adopt? Should we, as the Philippines 2000 program says, catch up with the NICs and make the industrial sector and its value-systems the dominant sector of our economy? Or should we follow the footsteps of the U.S., beyond the industrial stage? Should we, in fact, leapfrog industrialization, transform our economy into an information economy, and adopt in full the concepts of intellectual property rights? Or should we remain a predominantly agricultural economy as we had been in the past, living in blissful harmony with nature?

The answer, to me, is none of the above. The answer is to attain a balanced and harmonious development of the three sectors, all of which are important to us. We must also learn to be proficient in each of the value-systems that emerge from them, selecting what appears to be good and rejecting what appears to be bad.

To adopt three conflicting world-views – is this at all possible? I would compare this to speaking three different languages. We can become fluent in speaking English, Tagalog, and Cebuano. Fluency comes from a mastery of each of the languages, and internalizing their structure, grammar, vocabulary, and idioms. To speak a mish-mash of English, Tagalog, and Cebuano words is not fluency in the three languages; it shows lack of mastery in any of the three. We must be able to shift effortlessly from one language to another, depending on the situation, the location, and the people. Perhaps, by personal preference, or by accident of birth or family, we are more fluent in one than in another, but we must know enough to be accepted by native speakers of the three.

The ideal person, and by extension, the ideal society, for me, is one that speaks these three languages fluently and knows when to use one language and value-system, and when to use the other.

This can happen on a wide-scale only if our economy itself reflected the balanced and harmonious development of the agriculture, industrial and information sectors.

7. Towards a political economy of information

We are all familiar with the typical story of an isolated village at the edge of the forest. Some villagers have to go to town to buy a few necessities, and maybe to stock the village store. Others need to go to sell some products for cash. Villagers start to feel that the foot path to town is insufficient for their needs.

Village activists may even pursue the issue and organize the people to demand a better road. Eventually, public opinion is swayed, and a petition is submitted. The government, the villagers are pleasantly surprised, is amenable to the idea. Road-building eventually starts.

As completion date nears, the village organizes a welcome party for the first vehicle that is coming in. A few days later, the village wakes up to the rumble of engines and smell of diesel exhaust. The vehicles have come. And they are logging trucks, carrying men with chain saws.

Who needs the highway that is under construction?

We have all heard of the marvelous information highway and the miracles that it is supposed to bring.

In this context, we all live in a village at the edge of the forest. We know about the benefits we might be able to get by

---

This paper was presented in an international workshop on "NGO Documentation and Email Networks" held by Interdoc and the Documentation for Action Groups in Asia (DAGA) on November 27 – December 2, 1995 in Bangkok, Thailand. It has been reprinted several times (see, for instance, LIP #6, Aug.-Sep. 1997, p.5; Kapatiran, Dec. 1999, p. 15; Entwicklungs-Politik, June 2002).

bringing the highway to the edge of the forest, to our village. Some of us have even led the effort to build the road that will connect our village to that highway. But are we aware of the problems and are we prepared to handle the threats that this highway will pose to our village?

Had the village in the story been better informed – or more wary – they could have learned about the logging concession covering much of their forest. In fact, they could have organized with neighboring villages to oppose and stop the logging concession, which turned out to be a bigger issue than the road itself.

Like the logging road, the information superhighways are being built not because we in the village need them, nor because we asked for them. They are being built because they are needed by the equivalent of logging concessionaires, who have staked huge prior claims over wide tracts of forests they want to harvest.

To see the forces behind these information highways, we need to go back and analyze the history of the foremost information economy of today, from which much of the global information superhighway emanates. We need to look at the economy of the United States.

The transformation of the U.S. economy

It was sociologist Daniel Bell who first pointed out that the United States was moving towards what he called a "post-industrial" economy. The new stage has been variously called a "service" economy, a "knowledge-based" economy, and a "technocratic" economy. We now know that Daniel Bell was describing the emergence of what we call the information economy.

In 1956, for the first time, white-collar workers outnumbered blue-collar workers in the United States. In 1967, the information sector accounted for 46% of the U.S. GNP and 53% of the income earned. In the 70's only 10% of new U.S. jobs were provided by the goods-producing sector. By 1983, only 12% of the U.S. population was directly engaged in manufacturing activities, while 65% was engaged in information work. In the 90's recent statistics reveal the growing pervasiveness of the information sector. In 1994, for example, more data calls than voice calls were being made over the U.S. telephone system. This year (1995), it is expected that, for the first time, more electronic mail will be sent than postal mail.

Indeed, today, there is no doubt that the information sector dominates the U.S. economy. It is the leading sector in employment, growth, and exports. Increasingly, it is also becoming the strongest voice in U.S. politics. More and more, the domestic and international agenda of the U.S. government are being set by spokesmen and representatives neither of the agricultural nor the industrial but of the information sector.

Eventually, we can expect that more business transactions will be done on the Internet than on any other medium. When that time comes, the dominance of the information sector will be complete.

This is a basic, fundamental transformation within the U.S. economy. This transformation is the engine that drives today's globalization. From it emanates the intent and the funds to build information highways that will reach the remotest corners of the globe.

It is now necessary, to give us better insight into the nature of information economies, to analyze in deeper detail this type of good called information.

Let me quickly give some examples of what we call information goods:

Books. Music and videos. Software. Inventions, designs, and ideas. Genetic information.

Many would be surprised by the inclusion of genetic information in this list. However, genetic information has all the qualities of information. It is non-material, and it is easily duplicated.

Some special qualities of information goods

Information goods have a special quality. They don't wear out. They are not used up. One can give them away without losing them. Information is non-material. Electronic information is easily copied, and it doesn't cost much to copy.

Most important of these is the low cost of duplication. This is most easily seen in computer software, where the cost of copying a diskette is nearly zero. It is also obvious for music and video tapes. Duplicating a book may be more expensive, but new technologies now make it possible to scan a book, generate an equivalent text file, and then duplicate the text file at very little cost. As soon as information is converted into electronic form, the marginal cost of another copy becomes nearly zero. It can be broadcast over the radio spectrum or disseminated over the Internet at essentially zero cost per copy.

What is the implication of near-zero duplication cost? It means that people tend to freely share information. Many people have taken an altruistic view towards information: I won't lose anything if I share my copy; why should I deny it from one who needs it? In fact, the right to exchange information freely is considered a basic right. The Internet, for instance, began with a culture of freely sharing information. It is this culture which enabled it to spread into many countries who were attracted by the availability of so much freely accessible information. Even today, there is a very strong culture of free sharing on the Internet.

On the other hand, if one were able to sell the same copies of information, the near-zero cost of duplication means that extremely high profit margins can be realized in selling information. This is the basic formula behind all successful information companies, from entertainment, to software, to biotech companies. This high profit margin possible from information products is the magnet that draws investment funds from agriculture and industry to the information sector. It is this shift of investments that leads to the transformation of an industrial economy into an information economy.

However, these two implications of near-zero duplication cost are in direct conflict with each other. If people could copy information freely, there would be no need to buy information, and it would be impossible to realize the high profit margins possible from selling information.

This is the most basic conflict with the information sector and within an information economy.

Three economic sectors give rise to three worlds

With the full emergence of the information sector, we can now identify three major sectors in every economy. These three sectors are the agricultural sector, the industrial sector, and the information sector.

The agricultural sector is the sector of living goods and related services. Here, we work with the production and consumption of living matter. This is a very special sector, which I personally prefer to call the ecology sector.

The industrial sector is the sector of non-living, material goods. This sector requires the most in terms of energy and raw materials, as it involves the extraction of raw materials from nature, and the transformation of dead matter through human labor and machine power into finished products.

The information sector is the sector of non-material goods. The goods of this sector have very high information content. Frequently, they are practically pure information, like the software on diskettes. This is already the dominant sector in the U.S. and to a lesser extent in Europe and other highly advanced countries.

These three sectors give rise to three types of economies, and thus to three worlds. Agricultural economies continue to have their agricultural sector as their dominant sector. Industrial economies have their industrial sector dominant. And the information economies have a dominant information sector. Almost 90% of information owned today through patents and copyrights are in the possession of the information economies.

The interplay between these three types of economies comprises the dynamics of the world economy today. It is an interplay that is marked by a mix of competition and cooperation, exploitation and dependence. The world economy is increasingly being dominated by information economies, and the major economic debates today reflect the conflict between the interests of emerging information economies on the one hand, and the newly industrialized as well as the agricultural economies on the other hand. Of course, secondary conflicts continue to exist between industrial economies and agricultural economies, as they have existed in the 19th century and the first half of the 20th century.

Trade among the three worlds: winners and losers

Let us look at the nature of trade between agricultural, industrial and information economies. Consider the following typical products: sugar, television set, software. Consider the products to be worth $300 each, therefore tradeable with each other.

At 15 cents a pound, an agricultural country needs 2,000 pounds of sugar to earn $300. An industrial economy needs to produce one color television to earn the same $300. An information economy, one the other hand, has to sell one copy of a $300 program like WordPerfect to earn the $300.

In short, an information economy like the United States can come to Asia and trade one copy of its WordPerfect for 2,000 pounds of our sugar, or for one of Taiwan's color television sets.

Yet, how long does it take to produce 2,000 pounds of sugar, compared to another copy of WordPerfect? How many Filipinos have to work, how many days, to produce the same value as a product which one person can copy in a few minutes?

An information economy can produce, with minimum of input in labor and raw material, exchange value that agricultural and even industrial countries must produce at considerable inputs of labor and raw materials. Another way of saying this is that information economies are in a position to realize huge margins of profits when trading with other economies; therefore, they are also in a position to extract huge amounts of wealth from their trading partners.

We can already see how developing countries are becoming captive markets of information economies. Last August 1995, the monopolistically-owned Windows 95 operating system was introduced. This operating system renders obsolete all currently existing PC software and hardware. All such systems are now considered "legacy" systems. Many of us have become captive to this never-ending cycle of software and hardware replacement and purchase. A connection to the Internet is not much different. The introduction of the World Wide Web (WWW) has made it "necessary" for Internet users to upgrade their 2,400 bps modems to 14.4 and then to 28.8 kbps modems. Now they are talking of ISDN, which will render obsolete much of the current crop of Internet access hardware.

Imagine the huge markets created for the information economies.

The emerging new colonialism

What we are witnessing is the emergence of a new type of colonial relation that can exist between an agricultural economy and an information economy, where the former becomes the source of cheap raw materials and a market for highly profitable information products. Indeed, this new type of colonial relationship can even exist between an information economy and an industrial economy, where the industrial economy serves as a market for expensive information products and a source of relatively cheaper and lower-margin industrial products.

This is a further development of the old-style colonial relationship between industrial and agricultural economies, which continues in many parts of the world.

This new type of colonialism will exploit agricultural countries even more as their genetic resources are considered a "heritage of mankind" and therefore practically free. It will ravage their agricultural sectors with patented genetically-engineered agricultural products of advanced countries. Even emerging newly-industrialized countries like Thailand or India can fall victim to this new type of colonialism. In fact, most countries are now captive to new binding agreements like the GATT/WTO, which provide the legal infrastructure for the world dominance of the emerging information economies by protecting their monopolies over information on one hand, and prying open new information sources (biodiversity, the professions) and markets (telecommunications, media, and services), on the other hand.

The special role that the Internet will play in this scheme is as the global infrastructure for the distribution of the information goods, which advanced information economies will be selling to the rest of the world.

Information ownership: Intellectual property rights

Information has one special quality: it is very easy to copy. This is true of books, videos, tapes, software, compact discs. This is also true of ideas, designs, inventions and genetic information. This is the basis of the extremely high profit margins possible in the information sector. When you can sell at $100 what you can produce for less than a dollar, which is what successful software companies like Microsoft do, you are bound to enjoy fantastic super-profits. But this is also the "weakness" of information goods.

Many people simply copy them. Recent technologies have made copying easier and easier. As soon as a new version of a computer program is released, it is immediately copied and shared by users from Manila to Moscow, from Hongkong to Honduras.

To preserve the potential for high profit, information economies must prevent information sharing. They have therefore developed an elaborate legal structure based on the concept of intellectual property rights, which are essentially monopoly rights, which gives them the power, backed by the State, to prevent the copying and sharing of information, to maintain an artificial scarcity, and preserve their monopoly super-profits. Those who own information goods through such a monopoly mechanism as intellectual property rights are the new rentier class of the information sector.

The monopoly concepts of intellectual property rights, which include patents and copyrights, are the main form of ownership in the information sector and in information economies. Together with the infrastructure for distributing information goods (the information superhighways), information economies have also imposed on the rest of the world, through GATT, a legal infrastructure for recognizing their monopoly claims over information.

The conflict between information economies on the one side and industrial and agricultural economies on the other side, manifests itself in this debate on intellectual property rights. Whenever U.S. diplomats and businessmen open their mouths, they never fail to refer to intellectual property rights as a major issue where they pose non-negotiable demands. Protection for intellectual property rights has become the number one U.S. demand in all bilateral and multilateral negotiations.

In fact, it is the natural spread of information, and the need by information economies to chase information goods, identify their end-users, and to charge these end-users for usage, that is the real engine of today's globalization. Whether information companies like it or not, information automatically globalizes itself as it is shared among people who find it useful. Thus information companies find that they must institute international systems of ownership, controls, and policing, if they want to prevent the free sharing of information and regain their profit margins over their information products.

Intellectual property rights, which is an issue about ownership and control of information, is a central issue in the struggle of poor countries against domination by information economies.

Towards a political economy of information

Let me summarize the salient points of this presentation:

1. The U.S. and other advanced economies have undergone a fundamental transformation in their economy, which is marked by the increasing dominance of the information sector.

2. Information goods have special qualities which make the information sector qualitatively different from the industrial sector. Specifically, information is very easy to duplicate. On the one hand, this makes possible extremely high profit margins. On the other hand, people can easily make copies for themselves without need to pay for the information.

3. Information economies have developed a monopolistic concept of information ownership, built on intellectual property rights like patents and copyrights, which declares it illegal for people to make copies of information goods for themselves or for sharing with others without the permission of the monopoly owner.

4. The world economic and trade agenda is increasingly being set by the world's information economies. GATT/WTO is the best example. Its centerpiece is the adoption of a stricter intellectual property rights regime, which institutionalizes a worldwide legal framework for maintaining the high profit margins of information economies, and the opening of the service and

agricultural sectors of GATT members, creating a vast new market for the information and biotechnology products of information economies.

5. Information economies need a global infrastructure for distributing their products. This infrastructure is now being built around the Internet, a huge worldwide network of computers and high speed data lines.

6. The dominance of the information sector depends entirely upon the high profit margins possible in this sector, which in turn rests entirely upon the monopolistic concept of preventing others from freely copying the information. This is the basic contradiction within the information sector and within an information economy: information-based companies can keep their high profit margins only if they can keep people from freely copying their products, but the nature of information itself leads people to share information freely among themselves. The form of ownership is in total conflict with the nature of the good.

A political economy of information would analyze the basic contradiction in an information economy and its various expressions. It would identify the new economic relations and classes that emerge out of the social restratification. It would search for the motive forces that can be mobilized to initiate basic changes in the property relations. It would identify the main forces, the reliable allies, the middle forces, and the opponents of change. It would study what demands must be raised to mobilize and unite the motive forces for change. It would then try to discover new property relations that are more consistent with the nature of information goods.

Developing such a political economy of information has become an immediate necessity, given the rapidity with which the information sector has established its dominance.

Part II. ICTs and the Internet

A common critique of the Internet says: "The technology is great. But it is only accessible at considerable cost, and to a small percent of the population. Until we make it more universally accessible and bring down its cost, few of the poor can benefit from the technology."

Such a critique sees the Internet – towards which new information and communications technologies (ICTs) are converging today – essentially as a democratizing factor. At worst, it sees the technology as class-neutral, which can be as useful to the poor as to the rich, once it becomes affordable and universally accessible. The main problem according to this critique, therefore, is to bring the Internet to the masses. Or, as some would probably put it, to bring the masses to the Internet.

From Chiapas to the Balkans, from eastern Europe to Indonesia, popular movements have used the Internet to reach millions. Email and mailing lists have led to the emergence of virtual communities. Future e-commerce offers tantalizing possibilities to small economic players for competitive advantage and huge markets. All these have enhanced the seemingly democratizing image of the technology.

But today, the Internet's reach in most developing countries ranges from less than one to perhaps five percent of the population. In the Philippines, for example, it is currently in the range of 2-3%.

Part II is based mainly on the author's paper "The Internet: A Deeper Critique," which was first presented in a symposium held by the Link Centre, University of Witswatersrand in July 2000 in Johannesburg, South Africa.

Optimists often cite Internet growth trends – a few percent a month in some fast-growing markets – to project that the technology will eventually be universally accessible at some future time. Then, according to this critique, the only remaining problem will be in reducing the cost of access.

Part II raises a deeper critique of the Internet based on the following issues:

- Rapid Internet growth immediately results in vast expansion of markets for hardware, software, connectivity, consultancy and other ICT services. Except for some niche areas like data-entry, abstracting services, call-processing and similar labor-intensive services, the information economies of North America, Europe and Japan are in the best position to exploit this market growth. (Chapter 8)
- The Internet reinforces the automation mindset that replaces workers with machines. Even the new jobs the technology creates are subject to this automation mindset, resulting in loss of jobs and job security. (Chapter 9)
- The Internet is a poor learning environment because of the intrusive preponderance of purely commercial sites, of its multi-sensory feed that encourages passive reception and discourages abstract thought; and its high addictive effect especially on the youth. (Chapter 10)
- The Internet is becoming more and more like television, though an interactive one. TV turned out to be an "idiot box" for many people. If it will be mainly an expensive interactive idiot box, the Internet won't be much of an improvement. (Chapter 11)
- The Internet's impact on physical and mental health has been largely unexplored in the public discourse. Problems with hands and fingers, with posture and with eyesight are the most common. But there are also incipient problems of Internet addiction and skewed mental development. (Chapter 11)

- The seductive powers of computers and the Internet are so compelling that they are drawing precious resources away from the major intellectual challenges of our time. The present era is faced with challenges like persistent and widespread poverty, the disintegration of societies battered by globalization, the flood of poisons into our working and living environment, the unabated destruction of our ecological base, and the loss of habitats leading to mass extinctions of wildlife. These are life-and-death issues. Time is running out on us. What are we doing about them? Are the world's best intellects working on them? Or are they working on Web design, Internet programming, or on-line transactions? The online world, including virtual reality and cyberspace living, are very expensive distractions from the real pressing problems that humanity should be confronting squarely today.
- In contrast to public spaces like the radio spectrum, the Internet has basically become private space owned by rentiers. The Internet also has deeply hidden centralist elements that negate its democratic and even anarchistic claims. Until cyberspace becomes part of the public commons, to move our lives into this private space is to fall under the control of a private matrix. (Chapter 12)
- The Internet also reflects an embedded globalist bias, from the widespread use of English to hidden subsidies for international communications by local users. (Chapter 13)
- The so-called digital divide is better described as a great divide between the promise and the reality of digital technologies. A good example is the way cybercafes are becoming centers of youth addiction. Another example is the emergence of a familiar hierarchy of privilege and power in the digital world. (Chapter 14)

8. Expanding market for information economies

Internet technology is very expensive: the hardware is expensive; the commercial software is expensive; connectivity is expensive; consultancy and other services are expensive.

In the Philippines, for instance, the cost of entry-level computer hardware has remained pegged somewhere around US$500 since desktop computing was introduced in the early 1980s. Users used to be able to copy software freely, but strict IPR regimes mandated by the WTO have raised software costs to the level of hardware costs, and often higher. A dedicated 24-hour connection needed by a network of Internet servers requires a minimum monthly expenditure of around US$300 for port costs alone to more than US$1,000 if leased line costs are included. One-time costs include the server, modems, routers, terminal servers, uninterruptible power supplies and miscellaneous equipment. Consultants, trainors and Web designers charge what the market will bear.

To get a better handle on the cost of various networking alternatives, let us see how much it will cost the Philippines if we wanted to make a specific technology accessible to the majority (i.e., 51%) of the population. Assuming 12.7 million Filipino families, Table 1 gives us an idea: (estimates circa 1994-1996)

Table 1: Cost of technology, per family and for 51% reach

Technology	Current reach (%)	Cost per family ($)	Total Cost for 51% reach (million $)
B&W TV only	43.00	100	102
Color TV only	14.00	300	1,413
VCR	12.00	250	1,241
Cable TV	2.00	1,000	6,236
Telephone	6.00	1,000	5,727
Fax	1.00	200	1,273
Internet	0.10	1,000	6,478
CDROM/DVD	0.10	300	1,943
Virtual Reality	0.00	2,000 (?)	12,982
Radio	84.00	10	20 (100% reach)
Total			37,314

Considering that many of the later technologies are often good only for three years or so, we are then looking at a social investment of several billion dollars every three years or so. And these figures do not yet include the cost of software. Huge amounts indeed for a government that lacks funds even to supply its capital region with potable tap water. For those who think these figures are overestimated: round the total up to $40 billion, and multiply it by some 20 Asia-Pacific countries, giving $800 billion, an estimate that is still below the $1.2 – $1.5 trillion that the World Bank thinks is the potential market for the information infrastructure in the region in the next ten years.

By simply participating in these new ICTs, therefore, we immediately turn ourselves into markets for information economies that sell or lease hardware, software, connectivity, consultancy and other ICT services.

So let us not kid ourselves, please. Most of these technologies except radio (and possibly black-and-white television) are beyond the reach of the poor. They are the toys of the rich and it is the rich who will be best positioned to make the most out of them.

What is clear from the table above is that to participate in these new technologies (at a level that will still exclude around half of the population), we will first have to turn ourselves into markets for the hardware and software companies of information economies like the United States. The attempt to participate immediately turns us into captive markets of monopolistic information firms.

By designing products with short life cycles and replacing their product lines every few years or so, these firms can easily trap us into a never-ending cycle of purchases and obsolescence. Equipment which break down after a few years are most often replaced rather than repaired – if they can be repaired at all. Particularly in developing countries, the repair equipment, skills, or spare parts are often not available.

Thus, investments in new ICTs – huge enough as they are – must be repeated every few years or so, not only to stay current with the technology but also to remain competitive.

A firm's ICT expenditure over time will therefore look like a downhill obstacle course: a series of large investments every few years or so, to discard obsolescent technology and acquire a more competitive new technology. Each new investment promises to give the firm a better competitive edge thru lower marginal costs.

Such a cost-versus-time expenditure graph may be seen as a series of huge expenditures, reflecting the high cost and rapidly changing nature of the technology, superimposed on steadily decreasing marginal costs, reflecting the improved competitiveness promised by newer ICTs.

The downhill obstacle course is a typical feature of elitist technologies: the entry costs are very high, but once you're in, the marginal costs are very low. The high entry costs filter out the many who cannot afford the technology and allow in only the privileged few. The low marginal costs make these privileged few much more competitive compared to the excluded many.

The promise of ICT – and the expectation of the firm – is that all these huge investments will make the firm more competitive and therefore more profitable. But will it, really? Perhaps it will, vis-a-vis those firms which are unable to make similar investments. But unless it has sufficient investment funds to leap over every obstacle on its path, it will remain less competitive vis-a-vis those firms who can afford the leading edge and presumably more competitive technologies.

Those with little money will remain blocked by the first obstacle, which is the cost of access to the Internet. They will be saddled with the highest marginal costs. For instance, they would be making operator-assisted overseas calls from public calling stations rather than sending email from their office or home. They would be going after receivables by visiting borrowers, rather than receiving credit card payments. They would be losing much of their margins to intermediaries. People who are unable to go over even this first obstacle will be living in a very different world.

But those who leap over the first few obstacles and join the privileged circle of ICT users are not necessarily in a much better position.

They will find themselves spread out over the obstacle course, depending on their financial capacity to make the necessary and continuing investments to keep up with the unfolding race. The poorer ones will give up after one or two obstacles, trapped behind an investment wall they cannot cross; the richer ones will be trapped after a few more obstacles; the richest will manage to keep going, becoming more and more competitive as they invest in each new and more expensive technology that the ICT industry throws across their path.

In short, the downhill obstacle course is a huge investment trap: a firm must keep investing on newer and newer ICTs if it hopes to make its marginal costs lower and lower to keep up with its leading competitors.

If everybody joined this downhill race, the biggest money will be made not by developing countries who hope to sell their agricultural or manufactured commodities over the Internet. It will be made by those who put up the obstacles on the race course: those ICT firms in the developed world selling the hardware, software, connectivity, consultancy, training and other ICT services.

It is these ICT firms who are best positioned to exploit this huge emerging ICT market.

9. ICT: job creator or destroyer?

Is information and communications technology (ICT) a net creator or destroyer of jobs?

This was the topic which more than a dozen scholars, consultants and union officials debated in an on-line conference sponsored by the International Labor Organization (ILO) in May – July 1998.

It is both

As expected, the discussants all acknowledged that ICT was both a creator and a destroyer of jobs. That machines and computers are taking over work previously done by human beings was something nobody denied. All agreed that ICT was destroying some types of jobs. But all likewise acknowledged that ICT introduced new ways of doing things, creating in the process new types of work which did not exist before.

However, the discussants could not agree which role predominated.

A job creator

Some discussants asserted that ICTs create new goods and services as well as new market opportunities and income sources. Thus, they stimulate general economic activity, which translates into more jobs. The new ICTs, they said, are no different in their effects from the industrial revolution, which enhanced our productivity and improved our living standards. Historical records since the 19th century, they added, showed that productivity, output

---

A version of this piece appeared in the column "Second Opinion" in the daily newspaper, Philippine Journal, *on October 9, 1998.*

and jobs have all risen together. Today, the argument went, ICTs help businesses save money, which these businesses then invest elsewhere, creating new jobs. There is even a shortage of skilled ICT workers.

... and a job destroyer

Other discussants claimed that ICTs are selective in their positive impact, and that they lead to unemployment elsewhere. When bosses introduce machines and computers, some workers invariably get fired. In many workplaces today, machines and computers are taking the place of human beings, who are then left to fend off for themselves. A 1994 study by the Communications Workers of America, for instance, showed net job losses due to ICT over a 10-year period.

Not even statistics, however, could settle the issue. As one participant noted, the available studies today are confined mostly to Northern countries and a few Asian and Latin American NICs. The present data are too ambiguous for a definite conclusion, and one can find data to support either position. It is also difficult to capture in statistics the effects of ICTs on the informal economy which in many countries, is a big part of the whole economy.

The discussions revealed two trends:

Working at a distance

ICTs facilitate working-at-a-distance. This could lead to the increasing use of teleworking, to which many workers react ambivalently.

It is true that teleworking provides new opportunities for women in the home, for instance, or entrepreneurs in remote villages. But teleworking also breaks up labor cohesiveness and weakens unions; furthermore, it tends to exclude the teleworker from traditional social security and other job benefits.

... and managing at a distance

ICTs also provide management with new options in designing work processes and the workplace. They can ask their workers to work at home, or they can gather previously decentralized functions like decision-making and put them all in one central unit, decentralizing some functions and centralizing others, in whatever mix they find most advantageous to the company.

ICTs have also made the virtual firm possible, an enterprise that outsources much of its requirements and relies on ICTs to hold the organization together, enhancing its flexibility, efficiency, and competitiveness.

Outsourcing also tends to transfer jobs from large companies – which become virtual firms – to smaller companies. What is a dream to corporations is a nightmare to labor unions; small firms are more difficult to unionize and tend to violate labor laws more often. One effect of outsourcing is labor contractualization.

Who decides?

The key, it seems, lies in the decision-making that leads to ICT use. Invariably, it is management which decides when to introduce and when not to introduce ICT into the workplace. Thus, the criteria for ICT use will be management criteria, not labor criteria.

From the management point of view, machines and computers are very often preferable to human labor. Machines don't form unions; they don't go on strike. Machines can be upsized, downsized, rightsized or whatever-sized anytime; they can be run faster or slower, longer or shorter. Machine outputs are more consistent and reliable, resulting in better quality and lower cost.

ICTs, therefore, enforce the automation paradigm.

Whatever is profitable

Where the use of human labor instead of machines remains more profitable, management will obviously stick to human labor. They can relocate where human labor is cheap and maintain control through ICTs and telemanagement. The logic of profitability, however, will continue to reassert itself; as soon as it becomes profitable to do so, management will eventually switch to machines.

It is true that machines and computers may require new skills, and therefore create new jobs (computer operator, technician, Web page designer, Webmaster, Java programmer, etc). However, this job creation is an incidental part, while job elimination is the intentional part of the logic of computerization and automation.

New jobs need new skills, are less secure

Also, the jobs destroyed are actual people with real families, while the jobs created are potential jobs. To qualify for these new potential jobs, job-seekers have to go through a long and often expensive process of retraining.

Furthermore, the same logic of automation will also apply to the new jobs that ICTs create – these jobs will also be replaced (by automated software, expert systems, disintermediation, etc.) when it becomes profitable to do so.

As the pace of technology development increases, the pace of job elimination and replacement also speeds up. Even those who might have the skills to acquire new jobs are under constant threat of replacement or displacement. (Can Pascal or Dbase programmers still find jobs next year as easily as last year?)

While the net quantitative effects of ICTs are still being debated, their qualitative effects are clear: they have made human labor more replaceable and jobs less secure.

10. A poor learning environment

I first used the Internet in 1992, and thus have used it longer than most local users. I've also been working with computers since 1979, again longer than most Filipinos have. I belabor these points so the reader may appreciate that my opinions about computers and the Internet are based on a long period of intimate association and study, and not due to ignorance of the technology or fear of the unknown.

I presume, on the other hand, that many of our education and school officials have only recently become – or are not even yet – computer-literate. I would imagine that quite a number entertain persistent doubts about the educational value of the Internet, but they keep these doubts to themselves for fear of ridicule. School administrators today increasingly feel compelled to install an Internet connection – however expensive – for their schools to draw in new enrollees. Thus, they go along with all kinds of incredibly expensive proposals for Internet connections and Web browsing, most of which will only make money for computer vendors and Internet service providers (ISPs).

Is the expense justified?

Does the Internet's educational value truly justify the expense? Would providing our children and our youth access to the Internet give them, as the marketing hype claims, an edge in learning as well as a headstart later in life?

The government seems to think so. One of its oft-stated goals, for example, and one that is blindly echoed by officials who think

---

A version of this piece appeared in the column "Second Opinion" in the daily newspaper, Philippine Journal, *on October 30, 1998.*

they are computer-savvy, is to provide every school with access to the Internet.

Parents are as much a victim of the Internet hype. In their desire to give their children the best learning opportunities and the best education, they buy the most powerful computer on the market, with the largest memory and hard disk they can afford, and the fastest modem available. Plus, of course, a subscription to an ISP.

I submit that the Internet is, in reality, a very poor educational environment.

Building a good learning environment...

What, in the first place, is a good educational environment?

Let us start with the University of the Philippines, arguably one of the best universities in the country. Let us imagine ourselves in charge of improving the university's educational environment. Here's what we're going to do:

On the Sunken Garden, let's build a huge mall.

In front of the School of Economics, we'll set up a year-round fair.

Behind the College of Engineering, we'll put a row of movie houses.

Behind the College of Law, we'll open several nightclubs.

By the way, we'll change the rules and allow teachers to sell things to their students.

We'll enrich the library collection with subscriptions to Playboy, Hustler and similar magazines.

Beside the chapel, we'll put a whorehouse.

You get the idea...

With these changes, are we nearer an ideal educational environment? Given these "improvements," would you want to send your children to U.P.?

... or destroying it?

Most probably, you wouldn't, because we have, in fact, destroyed the learning environment.

The Internet today is such a mixed environment. There are hundreds of thousands of educational and learning sites, that's true. But there are probably even more sites with all manner of attractions, distractions and temptations for students – all within a few keypresses or mouse clicks. Because of the Internet's increasingly advertising-driven culture, these sites are in fact easier to find than the educational ones; their numbers are also rising faster. Worse, these sites are so intrusive that they send us materials even if we don't ask for them.

Effective education and learning is helped by a relatively controlled environment, one that is designed by instructors, professors and education experts to maximize the acquisition of knowledge. If you want exposure to the real world, you go on a field trip. But even such field trips must be carefully planned, to optimize the learning process.

Used carefully, the Internet can be helpful for doing a number of things, I would acknowledge. But it is definitely a very poor environment for education and learning because it destroys the carefully-designed school learning process.

Five senses or abstract symbols?

Computers may impair thinking in another way. Their multimedia and video capabilities, with future promises of three-dimentional display and virtual reality, will provide an increasingly full sensory feed to the user.

Education means learning to work with high-level symbols. It means going beyond the level that is directly appreciated by our five senses, the sensory level, and thinking in more abstract terms. The Internet, however, is moving in the opposite direction. Increasingly advertising-driven, it is moving away from abstract symbols, towards the purely sensory level, the level that demands the least from its users. From pure text, it has gradually moved towards graphics, full-color, audio-visual, and, today, live video. They are now talking of three-dimensional video and, beyond that, of virtual reality using tactile suits.

However, engaging the senses totally may also encourage passive reception of the data feed and discourage imaginative thinking and highly symbolic thought, raising questions about the computer's educational value.

Internet addiction: losing touch with the real world

Worse, it also exerts a powerful grip on the students' psyche – in the same way that addictive drugs can. Today, some psychologists are already warning against the emergence of a psychological problem which is best described as Internet addiction – when a user begins to take the virtual world so seriously that he begins to lose touch with – or to stay away from – the real world.

Authors Russel Mokhiber and Robert Weissman, for instance, have called attention to a report, "Fool's Gold: A Critical Look at Computers in Childhood," released last September 2000 by the Alliance for Childhood, a group of more than 75 educators, child-development and health authorities. The report called for:

- a moratorium on the further introduction of computers in early childhood and elementary education – except for special cases – to "create a climate for a broad national discussion about the serious developmental risks" posed by computers in childhood.

- a comprehensive study by the U.S. Surgeon General on the physical, emotional, and other developmental hazards that computers pose to children.
- spending money less on computers and more on "proven educational interventions for children at risk of school failure, including smaller classes and smaller schools, higher salaries to attract and retain good teachers, and early attention to nutrition, high-quality child care and health care, and safe housing."

Some suggestions

If the government wants to improve the learning environment for students, as well as the entire population, it should consider the following options:

- Expand school and public libraries. Build more of them. Let us have a public library in every town, if not every barangay. Adopt an aggressive program to stock up these libraries by reprinting the best educational books and translating them into local languages.
- Implement a continuing skills-upgrading program for teachers. A good, highly-motivated, well-paid teacher supported with a carefully-designed curriculum and good books will beat the Internet hands down as far as real learning is concerned.
- Forget about cable TV, which needs a monthly subscription and which the majority cannot afford. Use the government-owned Channel 4, which is freely accessible to anybody with a TV set within its range, primarily for educational purposes. This channel has no business airing basketball games, soap operas, sitcoms and other inanities.
- Acquire all kinds of documentary videos through compulsory licensing, including the Discovery Channel series, and air them on Channel 4. Allow other channels to rebroadcast these materials.

- Form an experimental educational internet among schools which already have necessary networking facilities. This educational internet will only contain material that fits a well-thought out set of criteria for educational materials. Such an internet can draw materials but will be completely separate from the commercial, worldwide Internet.

We have today so little resources that it is absolutely necessary to use them as wisely as possible. Surely, we do not want to squander our precious resources on extremely expensive Internet technologies that must be replaced every three to five years.

Worse, the Internet will draw our students away from real learning.

11. An interactive idiot box

Many years ago, a technology was born that inventors promised would revolutionize education, raise to new heights the cultural level of millions, and abolish ignorance. This technology was not the computer; neither was it the Internet.

It was television. TV, claimed its original proponents, would usher a new era of low-cost access to education and learning for the masses. Today, the TV set is called an "idiot box." Those who expect the Internet to usher a new information age should look at our experience with TV. Television technology turned into its opposite due, among other things, to the following factors:

- Governments tightly restricted who may set up TV stations. Instead of allowing anybody with the knowledge and resources, governments made TV broadcasting illegal, except for the very few who got government licences. The original technology itself allowed only a few channels, and reinforced the elitist ownership structure in the industry.
- With few exceptions, many governments privatized the television industry. This put profit-making ahead of other informative, educational or cultural considerations. Even government stations had to justify their existence by competing with private stations on the basis of their bottomline.

This is the first part of the paper "The Internet: A Second Opinion" submitted by the author for an international workshop on "ICTs, NGOs and Developing Countries" held by Interdoc, AsiaLink and the International NGO Forum on Indonesian Development (INFID) on July 19-24, 1999 in Anyer, Indonesia.

- Those who controlled TV made it a marketing medium, for selling products, services, and life styles. All other content became secondary to hard-sell advertising (actual commercials), soft-sell marketing (shows and movies that sold a life style), or entertainment (whose captive audience was actually sold to advertisers), with occasional news programs or educational films thrown in as concession to public service.
- Compared to radio, its non-visual predecessor, television – particularly color TV – was a highly sensory medium. The technology could feed the viewer with sounds and visuals, with little need for response, interaction, or additional imagination. This turned the viewer into a passive recipient of program material.
- Television merged fiction and reality on the same screen. Coverage of real wars intermingled with war movies that were meant for entertainment; violent films were shown side by side with news about violent crimes. This gradually dulled the viewers' sensitivity towards real-life suffering and injustice and blurred ethical judgments about right and wrong.

Even before the Internet, computer technology had, in a way, already evolved its own "idiot box": concerned that their children were being left out of the computer revolution and fooled by marketing hype, many parents rushed out to buy the cheapest "computer" they could afford, many of which were no better than game machines. Their educational value was worse than zero; they exposed children to non-stop violence, distorted their values, led to game addiction, and interfered with real education and learning. Exactly the same trend is happening today with Internet cafes, which in many areas are fast becoming centers of child addiction to violent games and other forms of escapism.

Sometime between 1994 and 1995, the number of commercial sites on the Internet exceeded the number of government and academic sites for the first time. The trend accelerated as the U.S., where majority of the world's Internet sites are located, pursued a conscious program to turn over much of the Internet backbone to the private sector. Today, Internet service providers tend to consolidate into larger mergers that cover more areas, provide more services, and include more subscribers.

Before 1995, a strong culture against advertising prevailed on the Internet. Only "demand-side advertising" was allowed – the kind that offered to buy, not to sell, that did not create "needs" where there were none, but acknowledged real needs when they existed. The ban on Internet advertising is now long gone.

"Entertainment" and commercialism have long edged out information, education and learning as the primary driving forces of the Internet. While the text-only mode was sufficient for most informational applications, Internet technology has evolved to include graphics and multi-media, with quality that is approaching and may soon exceed that of television. Now, they speak of three-dimentional vision and "interactive virtual reality," offering even more sensory stimulation with tactile pressure suits. Their immediate selling appeal will probably be adult-oriented.

Indeed, the Internet today is sometimes seen as the television of the 21st century. Here's a summary of recent Internet trends that can help you judge if it is indeed going the way of TV:

- from small service providers to large service providers;
- from academic and government to business and commercial interests;
- from information and educational concerns to entertainment and advertising;
- from free access to credit-card access;
- from demand-driven "pull" to supply-driven "push" technologies;
- from text applications to multimedia and virtual reality;
- from long useful life to rapid obsolescence; and

- from days or hours to milliseconds and microseconds in response times.

It is true that the Internet, unlike television, is an interactive medium, where information can flow back and forth, and to that extent it continues to be useful, particularly for information searching.

In many sites, however, the quality of the interaction has deteriorated to simple "click"/"no click," yes/no, accept/cancel user decisions which are not so different from the "next channel"/ "previous channel" decisions made with the TV remote control. Web gurus today speak of "push technologies," that automatically determine a user's taste and preferences based on earlier selections he had made on the Internet, and then feed him with more of the same, with no additional prompting necessary. This will supposedly enable the user to go back to his couch, relax, and enjoy the influx of Web entertainment and advertising – making instant purchases along the way with a few clicks – just the way that he enjoyed yesteryear's television.

Unexplored physical and mental side-effects

How will staring at a radiation source several hours a day affect our eyesight? Many computer "techies" wear thick glasses and are practically blind without them. Will this happen to us too? Computer courses may soon be required in secondary, if not elementary, levels. Will it happen to them too? Health concerns have also been raised with respect to the low-frequency (in the 50-60 Hz area) and ultrasonic emissions of video monitors.

Neither would persistent reports of a link between cellphones and brain or ear tumors go away. We do know that high-frequency radio emissions at higher powers disrupt cell and genetic functions. What is the safe threshold? Is there any threshold at all? As the technology increasingly relies on mobile and wireless computing, these health concerns must be confronted squarely.

The computer's automation paradigm has another side-effect. When cars and other machines were first invented, we thought they were wonderful because they saved us a lot of physical effort. But people who depended heavily on them got less physical exercise. They became prone to obesity, hypertension, heart disease and other degenerative diseases common to modern populations. If reliance on machines for physical labor leads to physical problems, isn't it worrisome what reliance on machines for mental tasks could lead to?

People who have gotten used to TV, for instance, cannot anymore imagine other ways of entertaining themselves at home.

Computer users today are already complaining about how they have grown dependent on their word processors, unable to go back to paper and pencil or even a typewriter. After years of word processor use, the screen and keyboard have become an integral part of their thinking and writing processes; they are lost – unable to think and to write – without a screen and keyboard in front of them.

Do we really want to end up unable to think without a thousand-dollar machine in front of us?

12. Private space controlled by rentiers

The Internet will probably lead to changes that are much more fundamental and intrusive than the changes that TV brought about.

Today, we are being seduced every moment of our waking hours to use the Internet to conduct our lives – to teach our young, to buy our needs, to find new jobs, to keep informed, to amuse ourselves, to seek healing, to meet new friends, to find our mate, to search for God, and even to express dissent and launch protests.

Virtual communities, virtual learning, virtual democracy, virtual revolutions, virtual sex. Everything in cyberspace.

This is the promise.

The reality is different. The seduction is drawing us away from public platforms, where we are in a stronger moral position to insist on our basic rights, towards privately-owned platforms where any rights are constrained by the fact that we are on private property, leasing time or space from the rentiers who own it.

Going imperceptibly – and in some places nearly gone – are the public spaces, commons and domains where we used to conduct our lives: the public schools, public markets, community sites, public libraries, public theaters, public hospitals, social gatherings, public parks, churches, streets, town plazas and town halls.

The Internet, for a while, seemed like a fresh beginning for a public space, where people can socialize, work, transact business and govern themselves on a public platform. Whether it was an information highway or plaza, the image was that of a public facility, maintained by public funds and open to all.

That is nearly gone too. Much of the Internet today is increasingly privatized, controlled by the emerging propertied class of the information economy: the landlords of cyberspace, the cyberlords. They are rentiers who own the communications channels, the routers and servers, the service providers, the search engines and the portals and who rent out space or time to those who want the privilege of using their facilities.

Much of the public still believes in the myth of the Internet's highly decentralized nature, that it is not subject to censorship or control.

This is not quite true. The Internet's democratic and even anarchistic claims can be negated by at least four deeply hidden centralist elements that can exercise a powerful influence in the content and direction of the network:

Corporate ownership of the hardware and service infrastructures. Many of the Internet's communication lines, routers and servers, service providers, search engines and portals are increasingly being privatized. Those who control these facilities wield enormous powers and hold practically unassailable negotiating positions. They can easily force newcomers to shoulder the full cost of Internet connections and expansion; disconnect recalcitrant portions of the network; deny service to unwelcome subscribers; target specific Web sites for harassment; exclude network addresses from routing tables; and so on. Consolidations in the industry further concentrate these enormous powers into fewer corporate hands.

Assignment of IP network addresses. Without a network address, one cannot run the TCP/IP protocol that defines who is part of the global internetwork called *the* Internet. Much of the available class A, B and C network addresses have been cornered by corporate entities and the power to allocate the remaining addresses available for assignment resides in a few institutional and largely corporate-controlled centers, who assign many of these addresses in blocks to large ISPs who then assign them to smaller ISPs, in a very top-down hierarchical manner.

The domain name system (DNS). Nearly every top level domain name – .com, .org, .net as well as the country domain names

– are controlled today by private entities not accountable to any public but themselves or their corporate sponsors. Domain names are important in acquiring a personality in cyberspace. Thus, those who control domain name assignments wield as much power as those who assign IP addresses or who own the hardware infrastructure of the network.

Technical standards. These include communications protocols, packet formats, mail and document formats, sound and video formats, and other standards that make internetworking possible. Without them, there can be no Internet. These standards had begun life in the public domain. Many still are. However, private commercial interests have begun dominating standards bodies. It is likely that in the near future, they will be in total control of the standards and, by extension, the entire Internet. Among these interests, the most aggressive in undermining public technical standards and proposing their own are monopolies like Microsoft.

The Internet may appear democratic and anarchistic, but deep within its bowels lurk control elements that are normally unnoticeable while gatekeepers use them benignly. Anytime, however, they can be used to make life extremely difficult for a network citizen who is perceived to be a threat to these gatekeepers of the Internet.

Because of convergence, even media which rely on public spaces like the radio spectrum are now getting caught in the private maws of the Internet.

To conduct our lives in cyberspace is to step into a private matrix where our rights are circumscribed by the often superior property rights of the rentiers who own or control it.

And the more aspects of living we surrender to the Internet, the deeper we sink into this private matrix.

13. Perverse subsidies

It was appropriate technology advocate E.F. Schumacher, author of the widely-acclaimed book *Small is Beautiful*, who once said that technologies often carry a built-in ideology which is so deeply embedded that one can't have a technological transplant without getting at the same time an ideological transplant. Among the examples Schumacher cited were nuclear power and the Concorde jet.

To this list, we might also add the current darling of the media, the Internet. The Internet's design provides a built-in subsidy for globalization, and all Internet users are forced to contribute to this hidden subsidy, whether they like it or not.

Distance-dependent costs

Before the Internet, most telecommunications fees were distance-dependent, because the costs are distance-dependent. One paid more to call another country than to call one's neighbor. In fact, one often paid a lot more, because many governments adopted the policy of making international communications subsidize local communications, thus making communications more affordable to local citizens.

The trend today, however, is to reverse this idea that international traffic should subsidize local traffic. The reversal is strongly pushed by global corporations, who comprise a huge segment of international communications usage. They have already managed to push back international rates in the U.S. The lower

---

This piece appeared in the column "Second Opinion" in the daily newspaper, Philippine Journal, *on September 29, 1998.*

U.S. rates now serve as platform for pressuring other countries to bring down their international rates as well.

In the Philippines today, for example, international charges are going down, while local charges are going up.

At the rate charges are being adjusted, we may soon reach a point where local traffic is subsidizing international traffic, which can lead to a perverse situation where the phone companies make higher margins on poorer users, to subside the richer users.

Subsidizing international traffic

This perverse situation is already the norm among Internet service providers (ISPs), which charge either a flat rate, by the minute, or by kilobyte, regardless of destination. Whatever the scheme, an email to another user on one's server costs as much as an email to a business contact on the other side of the world. Accessing your own server's website costs as much as accessing a website anywhere else.

Yet, Internet traffic within the same ISP definitely uses less resources than international traffic. If the costs were properly assigned, such local email should cost less than a similar international email; and an email to a user on the same provider should cost even less, because it uses less resources. Yet, the charges are the same – a clear case of local traffic subsidizing international traffic, a hidden subsidy for globalization.

ISPs don't charge lower for local traffic because distinguishing by destination for accounting purposes would cost too high; it is cheaper to charge the same rate regardless of destination.

Built-in bias vs. local

Here is a technology with a built-in bias against the local in favor of the global, whose very design spares the global the burden of paying for the full cost of its communications, makes it impossible for the local to use its natural competitive advantage of nearness, and forces the local to subsidize the global.

Although local Internet traffic uses fewer resources than international Internet traffic, most efforts to reflect this in a charging scheme have failed so far, reflecting a rather deeply-embedded bias for globalization within the core of Internet technology.

Thus, hidden in the Internet's design is a built-in subsidy for globalization; all Internet users are forced to give to this hidden subsidy, whether they like it or not.

Today, various media, communications and data technologies are converging towards a single Internet backbone. So, it is not far-fetched to assume that similar hidden subsidies for globalization – together with the monoculture that it carries – will soon emerge in telephony and the media, if they are not in fact already in place.

Biased taxation too

If you think about it, such subsidy is also emerging in taxation. Because we joined GATT/WTO, import tariffs (a tax on products made abroad) are going down and will soon be zero for many products. Yet, local taxes (including taxes on products made locally) are going up. What is this if not an emerging subsidy for products made abroad?

Schumacher was right. Together with technological transplants, we are getting ideological ones.

14. Internet cafes: connectivity for the masses?

Access to the Internet typically requires, as a minimum, a computer with the right software, a modem, a telephone line, and a subscription to an Internet service provider (ISP). In the Philippines, the computer and modem would cost some P25,000 (US$500); phone and ISP subscription combined would require around P1,000 (US$20) or more per month. This is definitely beyond the reach of most poor families, though perhaps within reach of the middle class, if they were willing to drop other daily expenses. At these costs, the Internet would definitely remain an enclave of the rich.

To make the Internet more accessible to the ordinary citizen, the idea of telecenters, more popularly known as Internet cafes, was born. The Internet cafe would take care of the hardware and connectivity requirements and a user needed only to pay a per-minute charge for access to the Internet. Typically, in the Philippines, this would range from P20 to P60 (US$0.40 to $1.20) per hour, with a minimum of P15 ($0.30) for a half-hour session. Although still expensive for the typical poor who might be earning less than P100 to around P500 each day ($2 to $5/day), Internet cafes made the Internet somewhat more accessible to the middle class and some of the poor who might need it badly for a specific purpose. Competition among telecenters would bring the cost of access further down, until the Internet became truly accessible to the masses.

I wanted to check this idea out.

This paper appeared in the No. 2, 2002 issue of Women in Action, *a publication of Isis International, a women's information and communication service.*

I was not a typical poor. For eight years, from 1992 to 2000, I had operated a small Internet-based service myself through a three-person outfit called Email Center, which offered e-mail access to the Internet, mostly to NGOs, non-profit foundations, cause- and issue-oriented groups, church and other civil society groups and activists. I knew very well the advantages not only of my own Internet account accessed from the home but of a 24-hour connection to the Internet where one did not have to worry about per-minute charges.

From a 24-hour connection, to access via cybercafes

In 2000, I closed down Email Center. Instead of getting a personal subscription with an ISP, I decided to do most of my Internet access via Internet cafes, and to try the approach that was supposed to bring the Internet to the masses. I opened an electronic mailbox (free) with a popular provider called Yahoo, surveyed my neighborhood for Internet cafes (there was only one when I started, there are around eight now), and announced to my friends and colleagues my new Internet address. On the average, I accessed my mailbox two to four times a week.

The first thing I noticed was that most of the so-called Internet cafes in the neighborhood were mainly game centers, where a majority of the computers were not Internet-connected but rather dedicated to running games. I found out later, as I checked out other Internet cafes whenever I travelled around the country, that this was true, with only a few exceptions, for most other Internet cafes I visited. In many cafes, the computers were often segregated; one side (or one room, in the larger cafes) dedicated to computers running games and another side (or room, usually the smaller one) for Internet-connected computers.

I would estimate that on any one day, one-half to two-thirds of the computers in use would actually be devoted to games. The remaining active ones would be split roughly evenly between online chat, word processing/printing, and browsing/email, with somewhat more engaged in chatting.

Internet cafes: centers of youth addiction

I soon realized that Internet cafes were not simply game centers. They were becoming centers of addiction among the youth, including elementary school pupils. I even started recognizing regulars in the cafe I frequented. They were youths of elementary or high school age but I'd see them at various times of the day, including schools hours as well as late evenings, even near midnight at times.

They were mostly boys. In fact, I could not remember seeing a girl at all in that typical game player position which was then becoming such a familiar sight to me: hunched in front of the machine, staring glassy eyed at the screen, with most movements concentrated on the wrist, in irregular but frantic twitching of the fingers against the mouse or keyboard. The gamers were in a fantasy world of their own, engaged in gory shoot-outs and sword fights with imaginary enemies or with other game players, and totally oblivious of the din and activity around them. In many centers, the rooms were filled with tobacco smoke.

I particularly remember two tragic victims of this new form of addiction because I knew them personally.

One was a first year high school student. Once introduced to the vice, he became a regular in the cafe I often used. Whenever I saw him, he was engaged in a game or watching others play. He would sometimes acknowledge my greetings with a slight nod, without taking his eyes off the screen. After nearly a year, he dropped out from the scene and I didn't see him again. I learned later that he had become so good at the game that the cafe operators gave him a lot of free time to keep him playing and attract other players to their cafe. By this time, he had stopped attending classes and become a full-time addict. Eventually, however, his parents found out.

Another victim was an elementary school pupil, living with relatives who sent him to school. He probably learned the game when some friends taught him or treated him to a free game a few times. Hooked, he started using his food allowance to support his addiction. The money was not enough, so he started missing classes, to use his transportation allowance too. Still, it was not enough, so he began stealing money at home. But the small amounts did not satiate his addiction. He was by then getting reminders and warnings from his concerned and suspicious housemates. One day, he took two thousand pesos ($40) from an unattended bag. Eventually, he was found out and was sent back to his family in the province.

Tricks of seduction

Internet cafes use various means to draw in gamers. Some offer lower rates during office and school hours or after midnight, when their machines are underused. Others offer bonus hours, like a quarter of an hour for every hour paid, consumable only after accumulating a full hour. To young people with a limited allowance to support their vice, every peso matters; so they take advantage of every offer.

As they acquire skills not only in playing games but in operating computers, they also try to make themselves useful to the cafe operators, in exchange for more free time. As ace gamers, they attract players in search of competition. As computer operators, they take a big load off the work of the paid technicians. I have seen youngsters of high school age work eight full hours as assistants to cafe technicians and clerks. Cheap, high-tech child-labor: part-time work in exchange for free computer time. Some of them work past midnight, working for their fix.

What kind of games do they play? Most games are shoot-em-ups: one walks through a maze and blasts every creature that crosses one's path; or one commands an army and deploys it to annihilate an opposing army. Scenes are gory: cut limbs, chopped off heads, and mangled bodies. To the young, however, play is reality and reality play. Mature minds may be able to distinguish which is which, but young minds often can't.

Right under our very noses, Internet cafes are seducing youths to a new form of addiction, corrupting not their bodies as drugs do, but their minds.

Unfortunately, students today are virtually forced by teacher and peer pressure to use computers and the Internet. Essays and term papers must be printed out. Forget about handwritten or typewritten submissions. Library sources are not enough. One must include source URLs. So, those with neither a computer nor an Internet subscription at home go to Internet cafes. There, they meet the high-tech addicts and are lured into addiction themselves.

Sadly, all this is happening while parents and teachers blissfully think they are securing the children's future through exposure to computers and the Internet.

Emailing in Internet cafes

What about my own usage? Were the Internet cafes useful to me?

I indulged in no chats and played no games. I mostly did my email and some occasional browsing. Two or three times, I printed out something.

But it was not the same. Emailing via Internet cafes tends to be quite expensive and inconvenient, because one is doing most things online, while the clock is ticking and every minute has to be paid for.

Downloading is slow, because the console's connection is not only to the local ISP, but to the Yahoo server somewhere in the United States. Reading the messages is even slower. Writing replies takes even more time, if one has to compose an outgoing message carefully. My friends and colleagues must have noticed a drop in the quality – and quantity – of my correspondence in 2001; throughout that year (as well as the last two months of 2000 and the first three of 2002), I relied mainly on Internet cafes for my email access. My messages were brief, hurried, and poorly composed.

The truly important messages, I would save to a diskette, to take home for further reading, a luxury not available to the poor. I would compose a reply on my home computer, save it to a diskette, and then upload the message on my next visit to the cafe. On some occasions, I forgot to bring the diskette along, or the diskette became unreadable, resulting in delayed or lost incoming or outgoing messages,

Browsing with notebooks and diskettes

I kept a notebook of keywords and sites I wanted to search on the Web, because I often could not recall all that I wanted to look for when I was already seated in front of the console. Sometimes, I forgot to jot things down on my notebook, or I forgot to bring the notebook itself. I had to save the search results to a diskette again, to study them more carefully at home. Sometimes, the diskette was damaged along the way, or my disk drive was not aligned to the cafe's drive, and I lost my work.

Three or four times that year, when I needed to do a lot of emailing and browsing, I cheated. I biked to a friendly office (the women's NGO Isis International) that had a 24-hour connection I could freely use, and had my Internet fix from there.

I have experienced the whole range of connectivity from a dedicated line to cybercafes. There is no comparison. It is clear that a hierarchy of inequality, not so different from wealth inequalities elsewhere, also exists in the digital world.

The social divide in a digital world

At the bottom of the hierarchy are the cybercafe users. They are the least privileged, extremely time-conscious due to the constraints and high costs and unable to use the Internet to its fullest. They are on the periphery, just barely on the Internet.

To get to the next rung, one must cross a huge gap, one beyond the reach of most poor: acquire a computer, modem, and a telephone line, and get a subscription to a local ISP, paying either regular monthly charges or through pre-paid cards. This buys one the benefit of offline reading and writing of messages, and therefore a huge leap in one's quality of correspondence. Browsing remains an expensive option, and one does it only when the data is badly needed. Like the carless middle class who would take a taxi only when one is terribly late for a very important appointment or in a medical emergency. A rung higher would be users who set up their own Web sites on a local ISP or on servers like Geocities, maintained through their local ISP connection.

The privileged stratum are those users with access to a dedicated connection, who don't have to worry about per-minute costs. With their marginal cost of communication near zero, they are the most competitive stratum in the digital world.

But this stratum has a hierarchy of its own: At the bottom of the hierarchy are those who are paying for "unlimited access," available in the Philippines for around P1,500 ($30) per month, but must still dial their local ISP for a connection.

Next are those whose cable TV provider also offers an Internet connection, at a fixed monthly cost of around P2,500 ($50). As soon as these cable Internet users turn their computer on, they are connected, usually at speeds that exceed the 56 kilobits/second that is the maximum, though rarely attained, over phone connections.

Then there are the dedicated connections, usually for servers that have their own Internet Protocol (IP) address, at a monthly cost of around P8,000 ($160) upwards. With a server with its own IP address, one is truly on the Internet, theoretically on equal footing with every other server on the Internet.

A familiar world of hierarchy

But even Internet servers have their own hierarchy, which is based not only on the speed of connection to the net, but also on the underlying topology of network connections. Today, and presumably for a long time to come, the U.S. lies at the center of these connections, followed by Europe. They are thus at the highest level of the Internet hierarchy. U.S. and European ISPs dictate their prices and conditions to ISPs of other countries who want to connect to them. In fact, Philippine ISPs that connect to the U.S. or Europe often have to shoulder the full cost of the connection, even if that connection is mutually beneficial to both sides.

Those who want to cross the so-called digital divide will be asked to spend much of their hard-earned money only to find greater chasms confronting them. While they may marvel upon entry into this privileged world, they will find that, due to their higher marginal costs, they are the least competitive among the privileged.

The poor may indeed cross the digital divide through Internet cafes. But they will be confronted with other divides that charge higher and higher fees to be crossed.

Along the way, they will find themselves in a familiar world of hierarchy, exclusion, escapism and addiction which keeps them at the bottom of the heap.

Part III. Genetic Information and Genetic Engineering

The information stored in the long sequences of base pairs in the chromosomes and genes of all living organisms are now accessible to those who want to manipulate them. The technology for doing so is called genetic engineering. Through genetic engineering, useful genetic sequences may now be identified, decoded, reproduced, synthetized, patented and commercialized.

Because every species, subspecies, and variety within species contains unique genetic sequences which may have commercial possibilities, genetic engineering laboratories throughout the world are now engaged in a race to decode the genetic information locked up in every one of them, and to stake private claims of exclusive ownership over them through biopatents. Thus, the world's biodiversity – the entire collection of living organisms on Earth – has become raw material source for the finished products of genetic engineering, which are popularly known as genetically-modified organisms (GMOs).

In a way, genetic information possesses similar characteristics as other forms of information, although its storage medium might be different. Thus, the same issues of low reproduction cost, the traditional practices of sharing, the trend towards privatization and monopolies through patents, copyrights and other forms of intellectual property rights (IPR) are the current subjects of debate.

As the world's genetic resources gradually fall into corporate hands, farmers and indigenous peoples' farmers and indigenous peoples may find themselves being accused of piracy as they engage in their traditional practice of saving and sharing seeds (Chapter 15).

Not content with legal documents like patents to establish their private ownership and control over the world's genetic resources, bio-privateers are also resorting to what is called "terminator" technology, to lock the genetic information in patented seeds.

On March 3, 1998, the U.S. Department of Agriculture and the Delta & Pine Land Company (now owned by Monsanto Corp.) announced that they had jointly received U.S. patent number 5,723,765. The patent covered a technology that will allow firms to develop crops whose next generation of seeds will be edible but sterile.

Since sterile seeds do not germinate, they cannot be replanted in the next planting season. So, the farmer will be forced to buy the next batch of seeds from the company which controls the technology. They are called "terminator" seeds because they terminate the continuous plant-to-seed-to-plant-to-seed cycle which supports most life on this planet.

Terminator technology works on the same principle as copy-protection schemes for software, music and video material. They disable the reproduction process and therefore create an artificial scarcity that keeps prices high, the classic approach of monopolies. They represent the technological method of control. Another method of control relies not on technology but on legal mechanisms, like patents and copyrights. But this method needs the active collaboration of the State. Many monopolies use both methods.

If used widely, terminator seeds will put the control over our food supplies totally in the hands of the corporations who own the patent to the technology or distribute the patented seeds.

Yet, by privatizing what has been considered for a long time the world's common heritage or the unique resources of communities, the biotech firms are themselves guilty of biopiracy or what is better called bio-privateering.

The worst case of bio-privateering is the race among biotech firms to collect blood and tissue samples from the world's dwindling number of indigenous tribes, to preserve their genome for future exploitation and commercialization. (Chapter 16)

Genetic engineering may also contaminate the natural world with runaway engineered mutants that may threaten our health and the environment. (Chapter 17)

15. Turning farmers into "pirates"

After we eat a particularly delicious fruit, my wife would often ask me to set aside the seeds. She'd take them back for planting in her farm in Quezon Province, where she usually spends the planting and harvest seasons as well as her occasional vacations.

Farmers save the best seeds

For thousands of years, farmers like my wife had improved their stock of crops by saving their best seeds for the next planting season. Saving seeds and sharing them with neighbors are age-old practices that form the core of farming cultures worldwide.

Today, biotech firms are threatening to redefine this age-old practice as an act of 'piracy.' Monsanto Corp. has just announced in a press release that it had successfully brought to court US farmers who had saved soybean seeds bought from Monsanto, replanted them and shared them with their neighbors.

After investigation for seed piracy, Kentucky farmer David Chaney reportedly admitted saving and replanting Roundup Ready soybeans, the engineered mutant soybean marketed by Monsanto. He also reportedly admitted trading the seeds with a neighbor.

Saving seeds becomes 'piracy'

Biotech firms claim that if they have a patent on a particular plant variety, nobody can save its seeds or share them with others without the firm's permission. By saving seeds and sharing them with a neighbor, Chaney supposedly violated Monsanto's patent on the engineered mutant soybean and engaged in seed piracy.

A version of this piece appeared in the column "Second Opinion" in the daily newspaper, Philippine Journal, *on November 17, 1998.*

According to the firm's press release, Chaney agreed to settle with Monsanto under the following terms:

- a royalty payment of $35,000 to Monsanto
- disposal of his soybean crop, with full documentation of the disposal
- inspection by Monsanto of all his soybean production records for the next five years
- full access by Monsanto to all property that Chaney owned or leased, so that the company may inspect, collect and test his soybean plants and seeds for the next five years.

Prosecuting farmers who save seeds

Aside from Chaney, other US farmers were also successfully prosecuted by Monsanto for seed 'piracy':

- Another Kentucky farmer will pay $25,000
- An Iowa farmer will pay $16,000 in royalties
- An Illinois father and son settled with Monsanto for $15,000
- Another Illinois farmer will pay $10,000.

All the farmers will also undergo inspections of their farms and production records for at least five years.

In its press release, Monsanto warned: "Backed by U.S. patent law, Monsanto is vigorously pursuing growers who pirate any brand or variety of its genetically enhanced seed, such as Roundup Ready soybeans and cotton and Bollgard cotton. The company has hired full-time investigators to follow up on all seed piracy leads it receives. To date, Monsanto has more than 475 seed piracy cases nationwide, generated from over 1,800 leads. Currently, more than 250 of these cases are under investigation...."

Patenting engineered seeds

Such is the typical modus operandi of biotech companies: they scout for seeds worldwide, engineer a mutation within a plant, and then patent the engineered mutant. The patent grants them monopoly rights over the plant variety, including the right to exclude farmers from reusing or selling the plant and its seeds.

In effect, the engineered mutant varieties become corporate private property, and no farmer can plant the seeds unless she pays for permission from the corporate owner to use the seeds. This payment for the permission to use is called a royalty.

Forcing farmers to shift

Biotech firms often argue that farmers will not be forced to use patented varieties, and they are free to use natural traditional varieties.

In reality, powerful mechanisms can force farmers to shift to commercial seeds. In the case of rice, for example, we have seen how the seed and chemical firms connived with the government to impose high-yielding varieties (HYVs) on farmers:

- The seeds came with a package of technologies that included fertilizers, pesticides, etc. If the farmer bought the package, the seeds automatically came with it.
- Government agricultural extension workers, many of whom sidelined for the sales and distribution arms of the seed and chemical firms, taught farming methods that required the new package.
- Farmers who refused the package were denied loans, irrigation, and other government support services.

Superior marketing, not superior seeds

Eventually, the HYVs replaced traditional varieties, not because the former were superior to the latter, but because their owners had vaster resources to market the HYVs and good connections with the government. Soon, the farmers had to buy, with every planting season, their seeds from the chemical and seed corporations which marketed them.

The same thing can happen to the patented mutant varieties under development. They can eventually push aside traditional varieties which farmers can save and replant, replacing them with patented varieties whose seeds the farmer must buy every planting season. Farmers who save such seeds for replanting can be prosecuted for seed piracy.

Once this happens, farmers will be at the complete mercy of corporations for their seeds, pest control systems, fertilizers, and other farming technologies.

In the Philippines today, industry and government researchers are now inserting patented genes into local plant varieties, including our staple crops rice and corn. Government agricultural authorities have announced that field tests of these patented, engineered mutants may begin early 1999.

Logic of privatization

Life patents, like Monsanto's patent on their engineered mutant soybean, proceed from the logic of privatization carried to its logical conclusion and applied to living matter. By privatizing life itself, biotech corporations have become privateers of the worst kind.

These corporate privateers, not the farmers, are the real pirates.

16. Beware of modern vampires

According to legend, the vampires of yore sucked human blood, supposedly to keep themselves strong. The legends about vampires may not be true, but some scientists now on the loose all over the world, who are engaged in collecting people's blood, may be worse than the vampires of old.

Scientists of the U.S., Europe and Japan have launched a project called the Human Genome Diversity Project (HGDP), which has become highly controversial. These scientists visit remote areas, particularly the indigenous areas. They might claim they are on a research or a medical mission. They might even actually distribute medicine. But their real mission is to collect human tissue and blood.

What for? The scientists collect human tissue and blood to look for genes which might be commercially valuable. Once they identify a useful gene or gene sequence, they intend to claim it as their own, replicate it in the laboratory, and then sell it in the market. This is the industry of genetic engineering, which is expected in the future to grow into a hundred-billion-dollar industry. Why the focus on indigenous peoples? Because they are considered – especially those who have remained isolated – of purer breed, with genes not found among ordinary folks.

This is the new interest of rich countries: to collect all sorts of living organisms (including human flesh and blood) in the belief that these contain valuable genetic information which, if unlocked, may be of commercial use. Through their advanced technologies, they believe that they can unlock the genetic secrets of life itself, to be owned and sold in the market.

The Pilipino version of this piece entitled "Mag-ingat: Mga Makabagong Bampira" appeared in The NMCL Newsletter, *Sep.-Oct. 1995.*

If you hear of some foreign scientists lingering in remote rural areas, collecting soil, leaves and roots, small insects, or animals, particularly those who inquire which leaves or roots cure which diseases, these are the "bio-privateers" – they acquire genetic information by stealth and privatize it.

Once they identify from a living organism a particular set of genes, they register it in their name through a legal instrument called a "patent," which gives them the exclusive right to use and profit from the genes that they registered. Even the people or the area from which the genes came from will have to pay "royalties," should they want to avail of the benefits from the genes that the scientists register.

Bio-privateering, also called biopiracy, is the new way by which rich countries extract wealth and exploit poor countries like us.

And the worst of these bio-privateers are the modern vampires of the Human Genome Biodiversity Project.

17. Genetic engineering and biosafety

Aside from genetic privatization, another important issue in genetic engineering and the creation of new life forms is genetic contamination from unsafe or unwanted mutants. Multinationals are now actually releasing genetically-engineered mutants into the environment—an extremely dangerous practice.

Industry, of course, has been releasing synthetic, non-living substances into our environment for decades. Often, it takes decades before we discover the dangerous consequences of some of these substances. This was true of radioactive substances, pesticides, chlorofluorocarbons (CFCs), carcinogens, heavy metals, nicotine, and even carbon dioxide. Despite all the safety claims made earlier by industry, we now know that these substances are a threat to us and to other species as well. Even when the dangers are already acknowledged, we still can not easily remove them from our environment. And these substances continue to threaten our health, our life, and our very existence.

Genetic contamination

While chemicals and radioactive substances are bad enough, at least they do not reproduce. But a microorganism, a plant, or an animal can reproduce, multiply and mutate by itself. Biotech companies – like the chemical companies that own them — can make all kinds of claims about safety of genetically-engineered organisms, but two or three decades from now, we are likely to find out that some of these mutants are not as safe as claimed. By this time, however, they will have reproduced, multiplied and perhaps mutated further, creating an irreversible and potentially disastrous problem.

Genetic contamination can threaten our health and the environment with runaway engineered mutants that cannot be recalled anymore.

What is the probability that these engineered mutants will actually fail and cause us problems? Can the engineering sciences tell us something about the risks from these products of genetic engineering?

Modifying a software or hardware system

When engineers design a system from scratch, whether it is software, hardware, or a combination of both, they obviously become familiar with their design inside out. Whether it is a piece of electronic equipment or a building complex, an accounting system or an airplane, the design is specified in a set of engineering drawings or equations, a set of building plans, full software documentation, manuals of operations, maintenance manuals, and other ways of describing the system's specifications, design and operations.

Even with such completely specified, perfectly known systems, if they are made up of thousands of components, or millions in the case of the most complex software or hardware designs, it is always a relief to the designer when the system is built or assembled, passes its final tests, and works properly, as designed.

And when a complex design is already working properly, modifying it to add a new functionality or feature always adds an element of risk, the possibility of introducing a problem that may cause a future failure in the system.

Often, even minor changes can lead to unintended and possibly undesirable side-effects. Some of these may be detected immediately, but some may not show up right away, perhaps only under certain rare conditions. An error introduced by a design change could lie undetected despite rigorous testing, only to show up under field conditions. This happens even to systems with fully known specifications and complete documentation, where we can theoretically claim 100% knowledge because we designed it ourselves from scratch.

Some systems are not designed for maintainability. This could be intentional or the fault of the designer. In such cases, even when the system is fully specified, well documented and perfectly known, it may be impossible to modify it without introducing problems into the system. In such cases, it is often better to start a design from scratch than to modify an unmaintainable system.

Consider, for instance, a complex piece of software. Every instruction and every line can be understood. Every line may be commented, and every module documented. The whole design can be fully specified. Yet, if the software is implemented with "spaghetti code", if tight coupling existed among different modules, if the rules of good design repeatedly violated, then such a program would be essentially unmaintainable. Even minor change to such a program can easily introduce side-effects ("bugs"). Such bugs can manifest themselves immediately or only under certain conditions. They can lead to subtle changes in the behavior of the program, or a major system crash.

This can easily happen even to a program that is completely understood and documented.

Modifying a living biological system

Biological systems are much more complex than mechanical, electronic or software systems. A soya or corn plant is much more complex than the most complex non-living systems ever engineered.

Furthermore, biologists understand little of the mechanisms that make living systems work. No design documentation exists, so the various considerations that went into the design are unknown. Biological systems come with neither complete specifications, engineering drawings or operating and maintenance manuals,

Even where genomes have been completely sequenced – the equivalent of decompiling software, i.e., deducing the source code from the binary sequences of one's and zero's – this is just the first step in understanding a biological system. The individual genes have to be identified and their function deduced. Genes, however, do not work in isolation. They interact with each other and with their nuclear environment. They lead to multiple effects, which are further modified by other processes outside the genome, with some results fed back to the genes themselves, creating an incredibly complex, self-modifying, adaptive system that is barely understood today.

An engineer looking at a genetic design that is working properly had therefore better leave it alone, at least until he has a more complete understanding not only of the system but also its behavior after modification. It is difficult enough to modify the design of a well-specified, well-documented system, how much more a system which he does not fully understand or whose documentation is missing?

Consider an organism's genome. Seen as software, it would have the equivalent of tens, or hundreds, of thousands of subroutines. They would form what is the equivalent of a very unstructured, unplanned program. Each genetic subroutine could be interacting with many other subroutines in a kind of very tightly-coupled, non-modular — even self-modifying — spaghetti code that software experts would consider impossible to modify and to maintain.

Modify this system – not well-understood, lacking in documentation, and poorly structured — and one will most likely introduce side-effects or bugs. Some bugs may show up immediately and these might be detected. But others may go undetected for long periods of time, showing up only under rare conditions. Some side-effects may be obvious and easily detected. But subtle changes can be missed. They can accumulate, and get noticed only when the system crashes.

If modifying complex but well-understood software and hardware systems tends to produce unintended side-effects and occasional disasters, the problem should be much worse with more complex genomes that are much more poorly understood today.

Modularization

To design reliable systems, i.e., systems that seldom fail, engineers often use the modular approach. We break a complex system into smaller, relatively autonomous subsystems (or modules). Then we create barriers between modules, to prevent unnecessary interactions among components in different modules, and to ensure that the interactions go through the modules' carefully-designed interfaces. This helps make engineered systems very reliable, with long periods between failures. The opposite approach allows any component in one module to interact with any other component of another module, forming one large humongous system. This approach has led to buggy, unreliable and crash-prone systems.

Biology has its equivalent of the modular approach: living systems do not exist as one humongous community, but as separate species, which interact only through well-defined ecological relationships. If species barriers are broken down, the unrestricted DNA exchange can result in a dramatic increase in the number of potential biochemical interactions. The probability of a problem from new unforeseen interactions rises rapidly, creating the engineering equivalent of a buggy, problem-ridden and crash-prone system.

Today's cocky genetic "engineers" are incredibly and dangerously naive if they think that the genetic modifications they are introducing will not lead to some undesirable side-effects, which may someday show up as genetic "bugs" and "crashes".

In fact, unintended side-effects have already been found among engineered mutants such as soya and corn, like changes in lignin content and impacts on non-target organisms and the soil. In software assurance systems, the discovery of a bug means that more undiscovered bugs probably exist. We can thus expect more surprises from engineered mutants in the future.

Genetic algorithm

The analogy between genomes and software goes further. Software have been developed using a method called the genetic algorithm (GA). GA develops software not by designing them but by evolving them, just as species evolve in nature. GA-evolved programs tend to be more robust than their human-designed counterparts. Random trial-and-error, it seems, can create systems that are more reliable than conscious design.

And if one is dissatisfied with GA-evolved software, one does not modify the source code manually, but reruns the genetic algorithm. In short, one does not add or remove individual genes but crosses the successful results. Even in software development, conventional breeding works better than genetic engineering.

When human designers analyze the final code generated through GA, they find it extremely difficult if not impossible to understand. The workings of a software product of evolution cannot be dissected and understood in terms of the structures of software design. The code is convoluted and mysterious, but not only works but it often works better.

If we can't fully understand the logic behind software produced by GA, how can we fully understand the genome? And if we can't fully understand the logic of the genome, how can we modify it without creating unintended problems? Clearly, the answer today is, "*No, we can't.*" Given that genes are part of living systems that reproduce and multiply, we are not ready today to modify genomes and release the engineered mutants to the environment.

Beyond human scale

Genetic contamination of the world's pool of DNA with synthetic ones creates problems, including the possibility of devastating genetic and biochemical catastrophes, beyond our control. We cannot stop mutants from reproducing, multiplying, mutating and evolving. They are truly beyond human control.

For these reasons, the manipulation of genetic information to create new life forms remains a worrying direction of technological development. The consequences of engineering new life forms are *beyond human scale*.

The same can probably said of nuclear technology, in so far as it creates deadly radioactive wastes whose half-lifes are way beyond the time scales of our own social existence.

While harmful, runaway software viruses do not threaten us in the same way that runaway biological viruses can.

The challenge of information and communications technologies (ICTs) is how to keep them from growing beyond human scale so that, instead of controlling us, they can continue to serve as a much safer outlet for the irrepressible human urge to experiment, to create and to control.

Part IV. Monopolistic Information Economies

This is the most theoretical aspect of the book, where some of the details of the political economy of information are worked out.

The monopolistic nature of current information economies hinges on corporate ownership and control of information infrastructures and monopolistic ownership of information through intellectual property rights (IPR). GATT/WTO serves as the international legal infrastructure for ensuring the protection of IPR and for keeping governments away from heavy regulation of information infrastructures. (Chapter 18)

The growth of the global information economy may be seen as the third of three waves of globalization. The first was direct colonialism, and the second the spread of post-colonial trade and investments. Historically, therefore, this growth can be clearly seen as a continuation of the long history of wealth extraction and exploitation of the Third World by the rich countries. (Chapter 19)

Looking into the information sector itself reveals a new class which has mastered the secrets of wealth concentration using new information and communication technologies. This class is the cyberlord class, which may be seen as the landlords of cyberspace who accumulate wealth by charging rents for the use of the software and hardware resources under their control. (Chapter 20)

The biggest member of the cyberlord class is Microsoft Corporation, controlled by the richest man in the world, Bill Gates. The political strength of this class is being regularly tested, as it flexes its economic muscles and uses its rapidly accumulating wealth to accumulate political power too. (Chapter 21)

At the core of these changes are the higher profit margins among cyberlords, drawing more and more investments from the industrial and agricultural sectors towards the information sector and propelling it towards dominance. The engine that propels that whole shift is the profit motive, which may also be described as a gain-maximizing strategy, or as a fetish for efficiency. In moral terms, it is called greed.

While many believe in efficiency as the main criterion for decision-making, an alternative criterion exists, which reflects better the coping strategies of the poor and of traditional societies. This criterion is reliability. Reliability, which may also be described as a low risk of failure, is best attained through another strategy, one that instead of maximizing gain minimizes risk. Lessons from information science, the engineering disciplines, farmers' approaches, and ecological principles also attach more importance to the criterion of reliability and the strategy of risk-minimization. (Chapters 22, 23)

18. Information monopolies and the WTO

Information goods, sectors and economies

The sector of an economy that involves the production of information goods may be called the information sector.

Information goods, being non-material, are quite different from agricultural or industrial goods, which are material. When the bulk of the cost of a material good is in its information content, it behaves similarly as an information good.

An economy whose information sector has become more dominant than its agriculture or industrial sector may be called an information economy. Earlier, such an economy had been variously called a "post-industrial" economy or "service" economy. Some people today use the term "knowledge" economy. The best example of such an economy is the U.S. economy.

Information goods are different from material goods as follows: the true cost of producing an information good is concentrated on the research and development (R&D) stage – in creating that first copy of the final good. Once the first copy is created, it can then be stored and reproduced electronically at very little cost. If digital format is used, then perfect copies of the original can be made very cheaply over unlimited generations of copies.

This paper was presented at the international conference "Beyond Seattle: Challenges for the New Millennium" held by the Asian Regional Exchange for New Alternatives (ARENA) in February 2000 in Hong Kong. It was subsequently published in ARENA's Asian Exchange *Vol. 16 No. 1 (2000: pp.57-63). This piece is a compact summary of the author's analysis of the information economy. Thus it repeats the core messages in many of the earlier pieces.*

Low reproduction cost

The low cost of reproduction of information creates the basic contradiction within the information sector. On one hand, it makes it very easy to share information products freely. On the other hand, it makes the potential profits from selling the product very high.

We share information all the time. The lower the cost of reproducing information, the lower the barrier in sharing it. Once information is released, it tends to have a life of its own and gets shared among users until all who want it have gotten it. This reflects the social nature of information.

But because the free sharing of information goods makes it difficult to set high prices for them, commercial information producers tend to do everything in their power to prohibit the free exchange of information. If they manage to do so, they can create an artificial scarcity, which keeps prices – and profit margins – high.

This is the whole concept behind intellectual property rights (IPR) such as copyrights and patents. IPRs prevent the public from freely sharing information and give the information producer the exclusive right to use, make copies or sell the product. IPRs are, in effect, information monopolies. Today, they are the principal form of information ownership, making high profit margins possible. The information economies of today are monopolistic information economies.

Investments tend to go where the profit margins are highest. The high margins in the information sector encourage the shift of investments from the industrial and agricultural sectors to the information sector. The transformation of the U.S. economy from an industrial to an information economy is simply the result of this natural movement of investments to areas which promise the highest returns.

Cyberlords: the rent-seeking class of the information sector

The propertied class of the information sector may be roughly classified into two: those who control the programs, the data, or the content (the software); and those who control the infrastructures, the servers, the facilities or the equipment for distributing, using, or consuming the information goods (the hardware). Both of them are usually rentiers, earning their income in the form of rents extracted from users. The rents include patent and copyright royalties, license fees, subscription fees, entrance fees, usage charges, technology charges and so on.

These rentiers of the information sector are the landlords of cyberspace. They may therefore be called cyberlords.

Cyberlords who control the software may be called information cyberlords. These include the owners of software companies, database companies, music, video and film companies, publishers, genetic engineering firms, pharmaceutical and seed firms, and similar companies who earn most of their income from IPR rents.

Cyberlords who control the hardware may be called industrial cyberlords. These include the owners of communications lines and equipment, radio and TV stations and networks, Internet service providers, theater distributors and owners, cable TV providers and operators, integrated circuit manufacturers, and other firms. With these facilities converging towards a single global information infrastructure for data, voice communications, media, entertainment, financial transactions, payments, etc., the industrial cyberlords are consolidating, merging and creating huge new monopolies that control large chunks of these facilities.

Cyberlords provide a social base for globalization. Because the social nature of information keeps asserting itself, information products tend to spread themselves globally as soon as they are released, regardless of the will and intentions of the producers. Cyberlords, therefore, have no choice but to globalize their operations themselves, to follow where their information products have gone. Thus, they push the globalization process incessantly to ensure that every country, every nook and corner of the globe, is within the reach of their mechanisms for rent extraction.

WTO: a legal superstructure for cyberlords

To strengthen this global reach, cyberlords need a global legal superstructure to impose their information monopolies and extract rents. This global legal superstructure is turning out to be the World Trade Organization (WTO). Under the WTO's persistent pressure, various international agreements have been concluded that protect and advance the interests of cyberlords. The most important, without which cyberlords would not be able to realize their high profit margins, is the TRIPS agreement under GATT, which binds all WTO members to very high standards of IPR protection.

Since more than 90% of all IPRs in the world are owned by rich countries, this highly protectionist agreement is clearly in the interest of rich economies like the U.S. and Europe.

The TRIPS agreement was followed by other WTO agreements essential to the growth and expansion of the information sector, and which have been or are in the process of being concluded. These include: the e-commerce agreement, the information technology agreement, and the agreement on telecommunications. These agreements ensure low-duty or tax-free transactions, an increasingly deregulated playing field, the lifting of restrictions to the entry of foreign firms, and other policies beneficial to cyberlords, particularly those who operate globally. These also include agricultural agreements, in so far as they ensure markets for the genetically-engineered agricultural products (which may be seen as information products of the genetic variety) of information economies.

Retaining the colonial trade pattern

With the emergence of powerful information economies led by the U.S., there are now three major categories of economies in the world: the information economies, the industrial economies and the agricultural economies.

Let us do a quick comparison of their typical products (agricultural crops like sugar; industrial manufactures like refrigerators; software programs or movies on CD). To produce $300 worth of sugar, one needs to plant lots of sugar cane, grow them for months, harvest them and then process some 2,000 pounds of sugar. A $300 refrigerator would need a lot of metal, plastic, glass and other materials, as well as sufficient energy to process and mould them into a working appliance. A $300 software on a CD can be copied within minutes for one dollar or so. Yet, in a WTO-ruled world, these products are supposedly of equal value. Clearly, the greatest returns will be enjoyed by the information economy and the lowest by the agricultural economy, with the industrial economy lying somewhere in between.

In the past, industrial economies enjoyed a favorable pattern of trade with agricultural economies. This colonial trade pattern kept erstwhile colonies under the former's economic control, although the latter had gained formal political independence. Similarly, we can expect information economies to enjoy a favorable trade pattern with industrial and agricultural economies. The high profit margins of information products will allow information economies to continue to extract large amounts of resources from developing agricultural and industrial economies. Agricultural economies which are trying very hard to industrialize in the hope of extricating themselves from the colonial trade pattern with their industrial trade partners will not necessarily succeed in doing so. By the time they reach industrial status, the U.S. and Europe will have become full-blown information economies, thereby remaining in a very good position to continue such a colonial trade pattern.

Historically, therefore, the emergence of the global information economy can be seen as the third wave of a continuing globalization process. The first wave involved direct conquest through colonialism. The second consists of the post-colonial expansion of industrial economies producing material goods. The third is the emergence of the global information economy.

High initial costs filter out the poor

Will new ICTs make it possible for poor countries to catch up with developed countries, or will they exacerbate the existing gap between rich and poor countries, and between the rich and poor sectors in every country?

The initial costs of entry (R&D costs, equipment cost, leased line cost) are high, but the operating or recurring costs are low (the cost of reproducing software, running equipment, using a least line). Because initial costs are high, few firms or individuals can afford them. These high initial costs serve as barrier, filtering out those who have little or no capital. But the rich who can afford the high initial costs then enjoy low marginal costs. This makes them much more competitive vis-‡-vis those who have been excluded from the new ICTs because of the high initial costs. The more competitive rich will get richer, the less competitive poor will get poorer.

Low-friction capitalism and the wealth gap

Software and information content can move around the world much more quickly than refrigerators or bags of sugar. The non-material products of the information sector can move more easily, much faster, and with less overhead costs. The same infrastructure for quickly moving information products can also serve for payments. The cost of transactions will go down dramatically. This makes possible what may be called low-friction capitalism. Low friction means less resistance to movement; information goods and money can move faster. The higher velocity of goods and money speeds up the various capitalist processes of acquisition, accumulation, competition, concentration, and the emergence of monopolies. Thus, the evolution from a multiplicity of small producers towards a few giant monopolies occurs much faster. The rich will get richer, and the poor will get poorer faster too.

Social change advocates who work in the agricultural and industrial sectors must grasp how the information sector and the emerging global information economy are qualitatively different from the material sectors of the economy. Only an appreciation of these new features can lead to an effective strategy against the increasingly powerful cyberlord class.

A strategy against cyberlords

Such a strategy may be summed up as follows: oppose privatization and fight for public domain information content, tools, facilities and infrastructure.

We should yield no ground to the cyberlords' efforts to increasingly privatize information, culture, knowledge and other non-material goods – including what are currently public domain material – through IPRs. This is the key struggle in the information sector. Information cyberlords will rise or fall depending on how this struggle turns out. In the software field, this is best done through the expansion of various forms of compulsory licensing of commercial information products and the protection of the people's freedom to use, share, and modify information tools and content. A strong campaign must be mounted against the patenting of life forms. We should propose non-monopolistic rewards for intellectual activity and the social sharing of non-material goods.

We should advocate various forms of community/public control or ownership over backbone information facilities and infrastructures, to minimize private rent-seeking through corporate control over such commonly used facilities.

Such a strategy runs squarely against WTO principles, which are highly protectionist over IPRs and which favor corporate control over information facilities. As the legal infrastructure which cyberlords rely on for maintaining their high profit margins, the WTO will remain a major arena of struggle in the information sector. The setback WTO suffered as a result of the Seattle protests has opened some windows of opportunity to question the various pro-cyberlord WTO agreements, particularly TRIPS. Developing countries must try to get these agreements postponed, reviewed, and modified, to weaken pro-cyberlord provisions and strengthen those provisions that increase public access and control over information content and facilities.

While the cyberlord class has become increasingly powerful, the source of its power is also the key to its weakness. This is the extremely low cost of reproducing information, which is the basis of the social nature of these goods. It is impossible to stop people from sharing information, regardless of the will of information producers and cyberlords.

The more freely people share information, the weaker information monopolies will become.

Our future: neo-slaves or free citizens?

The resolution of this conflict cannot occur separately from other ongoing struggles in the agricultural and industrial arenas. Only a combination of demands involving the three major sectors can draw the support of the majority of the people in these sectors and bring about a new political structure that is in closer harmony with the social nature of information.

How we confront this extension of colonialism will determine whether our children and grandchildren will live as neo-slaves under a system as cruel and heartless as the colonial system of old, or as free citizens living in communities where knowledge and culture are again freely-shared social assets, where industrial machinery is appropriately designed to serve and not to enslave human labor, and where ecology is the organizing principle in agriculture.

19. Globalization: the third wave

Our common colonial experience

Today's debates about globalization recall our experience against colonialism. We are all familiar with the latter. The dates may have varied; the colonizing country may have been different; but the main features of our common colonial experience were basically the same:

Using superior military might, the colonizing powers forcibly imposed their rule over our peoples, at great cost to us in terms of human lives and suffering and in terms of human and natural ecology.

Military conquest was very often preceded – and most certainly followed – by the imposition of new religions and cultures, which facilitated subjugation by dulling the impulse to resist or diluting the desire to free ourselves from colonial clutches. The effects of such cultural implantation on our minds have lingered and continued to do their damage, keeping us in mental bondage long after the last colonizing soldier had left our soil. Soon, the colonial mind started to take for real the masks worn by the colonizers and the words they used to deceive their victims, such as "we bring you Christianity"; "we bring you civilization"; and "we will teach you democracy."

This paper was presented at the international conference on "Colonialism To Globalization: Five Centuries After Vasco da Gama," held at the Indian Social Institute (ISI) on February 2-6, 1998, in New Delhi, India. A shorter version was presented at the Asian workshop for NGO Network Managers on "Gearing Up for the Information Superhighway," held by the Asian NGO Coalition (ANGOC) in February 1998 in Los BaÒos, Laguna, in the Philippines.

As soon as resistance was quelled, the colonizing power set up a colonial administration run at lower levels by people culled from local elites, many of whom decided to work hand-in-hand with their colonial masters to preserve their wealth and privileges.

The colonial bureaucracy then began the process of drawing out our wealth. Over the centuries, the colonizing powers enriched themselves immensely by drawing human and natural resources from our lands – human slaves, indentured labor, tributes, precious metals and other minerals, logs and lumber, colonial crops cultivated on seized indigenous lands, and so on. At the very foundations of the richest countries of today, are the broken remains of our own ancestors and the wealth plundered from their communities.

The colonizers brought with them the practices of plantation agriculture, large-scale logging, large-scale mining, and other powerfully destructive technologies, which were meant for plunder and for maximizing exploitation and profits. These unsustainable practices replaced the sustainable indigenous practices our pre-colonial peoples had relied on for centuries.

The impact on the people and their communities was grievous. We lost our right to self-determination, our freedoms and our wealth. Our best lands were seized for colonial tillage. Indigenous communities lost their rights to their lands. The impact on nature was equally disastrous. Colonial occupation was invariably marked with plunder of our natural resources and the introduction of monoculture in direct contrast to the much more sustainable and ecological practices of our pre-colonial past.

During this period, the colonial powers that took over the globe were mercantilist and, later, early industrial powers. Often operating their own State monopoly corporations, they scoured the globe in search of slaves, tradeable goods or raw materials, and bases for their colonial operations.

This period of colonialism may be called the first wave of globalization.

A range of anti-colonial responses

The independence struggles waged by our peoples in response to this wave of globalization are also familiar to all students of history.

Many of these independence struggles were eventually resolved through successful armed revolutions. We in the Philippines, for instance, commemorated in 1996 the centennial of our own revolution against Spain – one of the first of the national independence movements that eventually emerged in this part of the globe. Similar armed struggles erupted in Indonesia and China.

In countries like Malaysia and India, colonial forces peacefully withdrew and turned over formal political power to the local elites, who often retained the same colonial set of laws, bureaucracy and armed forces that had served the foreign masters. Again recalling our own experience, the United States used superior military power to wage a genocidal war against us in 1898, aborting the newly-born Philippine republic that had emerged out of our 1896 revolution, imposing an equally plunderous colonial regime on our lands and peoples, and extending our painful colonial experience for another half a century. In 1946, the Americans peacefully turned over formal political rule to the local elites, after first making sure that the 'newly-independent' Republic of the Philippines was bound by economic and military treaties that negated claims of genuine sovereignty.

Where independence was won by arms – in China, for example – the colonial economic and political interests had to beat a full retreat, their territorial rights and businesses lost and their properties confiscated and nationalized.

Where independence was 'granted' to a local elite which had been trained by their colonial masters, the latter nonetheless had to put up with some nationalist efforts by locals to regain control of their economy. These took the form of foreign ownership limits, profit remittances restrictions, local content requirements, export and import quotas, and other attempts to regulate foreign businesses. In the Philippines, for instance, foreigners were allowed a maximum of 40% ownership in corporations, and were excluded from specific areas like media and communications, natural resources exploitation, the professions, and retail trade. The latter restriction, by the way, exempted Americans by virtue of a post-war agreement they forced the Philippines to enter into, under threat by the U.S. to withhold any post-war aid if several treaties it wanted were not ratified.

The corporate counter-response

During this post-colonial period, the role of global capital expanded, partly due to internal developments in their home countries, and partly as a counter-response to independence movements and economic nationalism. Having lost direct control, global capital sought and became better at indirect control; military aggression was replaced by culture-aggression and economic control. By this time, internal developments within the colonizing powers themselves had prepared their economies for this shift: many of them had reached the late industrial stage of development. Huge private corporations in partnership with governments had accumulated vast amounts of financial wealth, turning money itself into a major commodity. These corporations needed new markets and investment areas, rather than colonial territories that were becoming more and more difficult and costly to retain politically and militarily.

We are also familiar with these post-colonial developments.

Again, they masked their real intention of drawing wealth from our lands and communities with such pretexts as: "we bring jobs"; "we bring technology"; "we will lend you money for development"; "we will protect you from communism"; and so on.

Instead of relying on military conquest, these global corporations worked closely with elite-led governments, particularly those local classes whose economic interests coincided closely with those of their former masters. Often, the local police and armed forces were flooded with aid, to win their loyalty and service.

The post-colonial bottom line was the same: the extraction of wealth. This occurred through: unequal trade (depressed prices for our agricultural commodities, monopolistic prices for their industrial manufactures); high interest rates on foreign loans; using loan conditionalities to exact further concessions; quick and massive profit repatriation; and low wages. By retaining control in the economic and cultural spheres, post-colonial wealth extraction could proceed unabated.

Chemical agriculture was introduced to intensify the production of export crops, causing widespread poisoning and damage in the countryside. Exploitation of our natural resources intensified, and energy generation projects such as huge dams, coal and oil plants, and nuclear plants in some cases were set up in the countryside.

A nationwide mass media infrastructure helped strengthen the colonial hold on local minds, to create and expand markets, and to ensure a friendly environment for foreign investments and foreign products.

The second wave of globalization

This post-colonial wave may be called the second wave of globalization, when industrial countries and global corporations would range across the globe for investment areas, industrial markets, trading partners, and sources of cheap labor and raw materials.

This wave has gone through several phases, reflecting the progress of an unequal contest between powerful countries strengthened by the immense wealth they had drawn from colonial victims on the one hand, and the newly-independent nations weakened by centuries of plunder and exploitation on the other hand.

The early-independence phase was often marked by intense economic nationalism, as local economic interests tried to enhance their economic sovereignty through protectionist measures, while global corporate interests fought to retain their colonial privileges.

The second phase saw a succession of crises that included the oil shocks of the 1970's, the debt crises of the 1980's, the socialist crisis of the early 1990's, and the financial crisis of the late 1990's, which is still going on. Socialism had earlier provided a counter-balance to global corporations and their governments, as well as a possible alternative path for independence movements. These crises weakened the capacity, the will, and the overall position of the former colonies and enabled global corporations to launch major counterattacks in order to regain much of the colonial power and privileges they had lost during the economic-nationalist phase.

The post-colonial counterattacks by global corporations mark the third phase of this second wave. This counteroffensive forced many countries to surrender much of their economic sovereignty to corporate-controlled international institutions such as the International Monetary Fund (IMF), the World Bank (WB) and the World Trade Organization (WTO). Through loan conditionalities, structural adjustment programs, and other means, many nationalist laws and provisions gained by earlier anti-colonial independence movements were undermined and dismantled. Some authors – Chakravarthi Raghavan, for example – have called this phase a process of "recolonization," a return of colonial privileges for global corporations.

The impacts of this wave of globalization are no less destructive than the colonialism that preceded it. Our agricultural products consistently suffer from low prices; our workers from low wages. We are losing much of our capital due to profit repatriation and the debt crisis; chemical farming is taking away our food security and putting it in the hands of global chemical and seed conglomerates. We are suffering from widespread ecological disasters, triggered by intensive resource extraction, disruptive energy projects, and toxic pollution. Our forests, mines and quarries are being quickly depleted; our air, water and soil heavily contaminated; and pervasive monoculture is seriously threatening our biodiversity. We enjoy national sovereignty in name only.

This part of our history and current events should also be familiar to most of us.

Alert: the third wave is coming

We are still in the midst of the second wave of globalization, yet a third one has already emerged. The third wave of globalization began to be felt worldwide in the last half of the 1990's and will probably express its overwhelming presence in full force at the dawn of the 21st century. This looming third wave is the global information economy.

Like the first two waves, the third globalization wave arose from internal developments within the hearts of the global powers. It is important to look at these internal developments, because they will, as in the past, eventually impinge on the rest of the world – including our own – often shaping our destinies and steering our development in directions we never wanted to take.

The colonial powers were mercantilist and, later, industrial countries in their early expansionist stages. The post-colonial powers were industrial countries in their late stages, when capitalism had developed further, combining industrial and finance capital into huge monopolistic conglomerates in continual search for new acquisitions, sources of cheap raw materials and labor, and markets. The third wave of globalization is marked by the emergence and eventual dominance, within the most advanced industrial countries, of the information sector – the sector that produces, manipulates, processes, distributes and markets information products.

There is enough literature that describes the dominance of the information sector in the United States. One of the earliest is a landmark study by Marc Porat, who analyzed some 201 industries in the U.S. in 1967. Here's an account of Porat's study (Megatrends by John Naisbitt, 1982):

"Porat sorted through some 440 occupations in 201 industries, identified the information jobs, and compiled their contribution to the GNP. Questionable jobs were excluded so that the study's conclusions err on the conservative side.

"Porat's study is incredibly detailed. He begins with the obvious sorting-out and tallying-up of the economic value of easily identifiable information jobs such as clerks, librarians, systems analysts, calling this first group the Primary Information Sector. According to Porat's calculations for the year 1967, 25.1 percent of the U.S. GNP was produced in the Primary Information Sector, that is, the part of the economy that produces, processes, and distributes information goods and services. Included here are computer manufacturing, telecommunications, printing, mass media, advertising, accounting and education, as well as risk-management industries, including parts of the finance and insurance businesses.

"But Porat's study goes on to deal with the more difficult questions that have overwhelmed other researchers. How does one categorize those individuals holding information jobs with manufacturers and other non-information firms? To answer this question required 'tearing firms apart in an accounting sense into information and non-information parts.'

"Porat creates a new information grouping called the Secondary Information Sector. It quantifies the economic contribution of information workers employed in non-information firms.

"These workers produce information goods and services for internal consumption within goods-producing and other companies. In effect their information products are sold on a fictitious account to the goods-producing side of the company. The Secondary Information Sector generated an additional 21.1 percent of the GNP.

"Porat's study concludes, then, that the information economy accounted for some 46 percent of the GNP and more than 53 percent of the income earned. This was in 1967."

This was also before the widespread use of satellite communications, fax machines, cell phones, cable television, personal computers and, of course, the Internet. Today, there is no doubt that the information sector is the dominant sector of the U.S. economy, making the U.S. the leading information economy in the world.

A global information economy

The increasing dominance of the information sector in what had been industrial economies is turning them into information economies. These emerging information economies – principally the U.S. and to a lesser extent some countries of Europe – are at the core of the third wave of globalization. Because of the way these economies are so closely interconnected, they are better seen as a single emerging global information economy. The Internet is perhaps the most visible portion of this economy – and certainly the one which has received the most media attention. This emerging global information economy includes the global infrastructure for telecommunications, data exchange, media and entertainment; the knowledge industries; the publishing industries; the computer hardware and software industries; the new financial systems that will support on-line transactions; the emerging global legal infrastructure based on the WTO, including the GATT and the agreements in information technology, telecommunications and financial services; and the biotechnology and genetic engineering industries.

Unlike the first two waves, the implications and consequences of the global information economy are an unfamiliar phenomenon to most of us. There are so many new things, so many new possibilities, that it is quite difficult to separate the chaff from the grain, the hype from the substance.

This is what this final portion of my paper will try to do.

Information: a closer look

Let us look closely at the archetypal information product: information stored in a magnetic medium. It can be software on a diskette, databases on hard disks, an audio cassette, or a video cassette. Remember that the product is not the medium but the message; it is neither the disk nor the tape, but their contents. The same medium with a different message is a different product; the same message on a different medium is the same product. Other forms of information, like books and other printed publications, live audio and video information, drawings and designs, and genetic information may now be easily transformed into their archetypal equivalent.

The distinctive feature of an information product is that it can be copied at little cost. The cost of copying books is still on the high side, but the cost of copying electronic data is nearly zero. Furthermore, we can give copies away without losing our own copy. This is true of software, databases, songs, videos, designs, and most other information goods – including genetic information.

In short, the cost of reproducing information – what the economist calls its marginal cost – is very much lower than the cost of initially producing the information – its development cost. The marginal cost of information is so low that it oftentimes approaches zero.

In the last analysis, this feature is due to the very nature of information itself. Information is non-material in its essence – a numeric measure of the uncertainty which it resolves. The non-materiality of information is the basis of its low reproduction cost, which may be driven lower and lower by adopting representations that can be manipulated at lower costs. With today's digital representations, the costs of reproducing and distributing information have reached historic lows – as low as the cost of copying a diskette or downloading a file from an on-line server.

Low marginal cost leads to sharing

The low marginal cost of information has two major implications: one for those who use it, and another for those who sell it.

For users, it encourages sharing. Many cultures, in fact, see knowledge as social wealth – a collective asset that is meant to be shared. These cultures – including most Third World and indigenous cultures – are therefore in close harmony with the very nature of information. When we share software, for example, we are only being true to the nature of information and to our own cultures.

But there are other cultures, where private property concepts have become more absolute and where almost everything has been commodified. In these cultures – often with capitalism at their core – information has become an object of commodification and privatization. Culture itself has become commodified, together with knowledge and life. They have become vehicles for profit-making.

Profit-making mechanism: the monopoly

Let us look more closely at the mechanism of profit-making through information. First, the seller turns information from a collective asset into private property. Then, copies are sold on the market, at prices set by the "owner"/seller. Once the initial sales have covered the development costs, the near-zero marginal cost of reproducing information now makes its selling price nearly pure profit. A diskette of software that may be copied for cents is sold for fifty dollars. A CDROM that may be reproduced for three dollars is sold for three hundred.

To realize these extremely high profit margins made possible by the low marginal cost of information products, however, the seller must create an artificial scarcity of the product. We have seen that information can now be easily copied by users themselves at practically no cost, creating a natural abundance which drives prices down. To keep prices and profit margins high, this natural abundance that proceeds from the essence of information itself must be prevented. The seller does it by acquiring from the State a monopoly in using and making copies of the information product, and by criminalizing sharing among users. This creates the artificial scarcity that drives prices up and realizes for the seller the potential profits from high margins.

It is monopoly that creates the scarcity. Such monopolies are euphemistically known as "intellectual property rights" (IPR), the main form of ownership in an information economy. They are the mechanism for maintaining the high profit margins of those who control and sell information products. IPRs have two major forms: copyrights (historically, limited monopolies covering literary materials), and patents (historically, limited monopolies covering inventions). In recent years, as the information sector gained dominance and the propertied classes of this sector increased their political and economic power, IPRs have been strengthened and extended to new areas.

IPRs are statutory monopolies. They are monopolies over information granted through statutes, by the State. Those who control information through IPR are basically rentiers: they make money by charging monopoly rents from users, who are threatened by State action should they continue to practice information sharing. In the Philippines, monopolies represented by the Business Software Alliance (BSA), in collaboration with the Philippine government, have actually raided educational institutions and commercial shops to enforce their information monopolies.

Conflicts within the information economy

Still, enforcing information monopolies is not simple. After all, information monopolies are incompatible with the social nature of information. The deeply-ingrained cultural habits of information sharing and exchange continue to assert themselves, regardless of the will of monopolists and their State protectors.

This is the dilemma within the emerging global information economy.

On the one hand, information itself is a highly social good; on the other hand, the forms of ownership are highly monopolistic. On the one hand, users tend to share information goods; on the other hand, IPR holders insist on their monopolies. On the one hand, developing countries need the widest access to various technology options at the least cost; on the other hand, rich and powerful information economies control almost 90% of all the IPRs in the world today, and want to increase their control further by criminalizing cultures that treat information as collective wealth.

The basic conflict within the information sector is the incompatibility between the highly monopolistic forms of information ownership and the social nature of information. This conflict is also expressed between users who want to share information freely and monopoly claimants who want to prevent free sharing of information. It is further reflected in the conflict between developing countries who need low-cost access to major bodies of information and information economies which have established virtual monopolies over information and want to criminalize the Third World culture of sharing knowledge and information. Historically, these information economies are basically the same colonial powers that have exploited developing countries over the centuries.

The socializing tendency emanates from the nature of information itself, and can therefore never be suppressed. The monopolizing tendency emanates from the potentially high profit margins in selling information and the economic and political power concentrated in information monopolies. The conflicts arising from these two opposing tendencies will drive the historical development of the third wave of globalization.

Internal engine

Within the U.S., the high profit margins in the information sector is attracting more investment capital towards this sector, away from the agricultural and industrial sectors. This is the internal engine that is slowly transforming the U.S. economy into an information economy.

Within the emerging global information economy itself, monopoly concepts are already well-established and are even expanding their coverage. One item, for instance, is always non-negotiable in the U.S. diplomatic agenda: intellectual property rights (IPR). These concepts are increasingly dominating international legal systems through bilateral negotiations with the U.S. and through the World Trade Organization (WTO). Thus, worldwide, pressure is increasing on countries with non-monopolistic attitudes towards information to adopt the same U.S. legal system that strictly protects IPRs.

However, the social nature of information continually asserts itself. Information abundance created through user sharing and exchange keeps breaking through the artificial scarcity created by information monopolies. The latest releases of popular software, songs or video immediately find themselves being copied in every corner of the globe. In effect, information automatically globalizes itself regardless of the will of those who insist on monopolizing them. Ironically, information monopolists find their products better distributed in those parts of the globe where they can not enforce their monopoly. They therefore insist on imposing monopolistic legal systems upon the rest of the globe, so they can realize the same profit margins they enjoy in their monopoly areas. Even one country that refuses to be part of this global legal system will pose a threat to their global monopoly, thus they will exert every effort to bring it in. These monopolists will never leave any country – or any community – alone.

They are the real engines of globalization's third wave.

This is also what makes the information sector qualitatively different from the industrial and agricultural sectors. It justifies why the emergence of the global information economy must be considered a distinct wave in itself, instead of simply a part of the second wave of globalization.

Cyberlords

Information monopolies may be established not only by staking monopoly claims over information content through IPR, but also by controlling the hardware infrastructure for manipulating or distributing information. This infrastructure includes computer centers, voice and data switching centers, communication lines, television and radio stations, satellite networks, cable networks, cellular networks, movie houses, etc. Like their software counterparts, most owners of the hardware infrastructure make money through monopoly rents, in the form of subscription fees or per-use charges.

Because they earn their incomes from monopoly rents, the propertied classes of the information sectors are rentier classes. They are the landlords of cyberspace, or cyberlords. The content monopolies are owned by information cyberlords, and the infrastructure monopolies are owned by industrial cyberlords.

The richest man in the world, Bill Gates – as well as several others among the ten richest – is a cyberlord. The economic powers of cyberlords are immense, and these powers are increasingly being felt in the political and diplomatic arena. Among U.S. negotiators, for instance, IPR – the mechanism which gives software cyberlords their power – is invariably a non-negotiable item in their agenda. It is the partnership between information cyberlords, industrial cyberlords, and finance capitalists which is the at the core of the third wave of globalization.

To sum up: an information economy is one whose information sector has become the main source of wealth, eclipsing its industrial and agricultural sectors. The products of industrial and agricultural economies are material goods; the products of an information economy, however, are non-material goods. The reproduction cost of information goods is very low. This has led to the widespread social practice of freely sharing and exchanging information. On the other hand, it also promises extremely high profit margins, if the seller can monopolize information. Information monopolies have become the main form of ownership in the information sector. The high profit margins that they realize have led to a continuous movement of investment capital towards the information sector, eventually making it the dominant sector of the economy and transforming the economy into an information economy. The products of this information economy spread worldwide, as people freely share and exchange information goods. Thus an information economy needs a global system for enforcing its monopolies as well as for gathering information materials, tapping intellectuals and of course collecting payments worldwide. This leads to the globalization of the information economy and is the engine of the third wave of globalization. The main propertied classes within the information economy are information cyberlords who control information content, industrial cyberlords who control information infrastructures, and finance capitalists who control investment funds.

First to third waves: a comparison

Let us compare the emergence of the global information economy with the two previous waves of globalization:

The first wave was after slaves, precious metals and lands for raising export crops; the second wave was after new investment acquisitions, sources of raw materials and labor, and industrial markets. The third wave is after sources of mental labor, sources of information raw materials, and markets for information products. This is why the World Trade Organization (WTO) pushed very hard to conclude as soon as possible the agreements on information technology, telecommunications and financial services.

The third wave requires freer movement of information across national boundaries. This has helped erode further the power of the State. While the State itself operated corporate monopolies during the first wave, and continued to be dominant over corporations during the second wave, it is finding itself less powerful during the third wave. Global corporations are now assuming the dominant role in the State-corporate partnership, in close collaboration with supra-national institutions like the International Monetary Fund (IMF), the World Bank (WB) and the WTO.

As in the first two waves, the extraction of wealth from the rest of the world is likewise done under a mask that hides real intentions. The third wave hides behind such phrases as "information at your finger tips," "world without borders," "global village," "instant access to the world's libraries," "free flow of information," or "TV with a million channels."

Behind the mask, the global information economy imposes its own global rule to facilitate the wealth transfer. The role of the nation-state shrinks, many of its functions taken over by private corporations. Global corporations continue to strengthen their political voice and clout, and directly enter into partnerships with local elites and local governments, often bypassing the host government as well as their own government. Corporate control of information, communications, and media infrastructures is strengthened through privatization and deregulation. National sovereignty is further curtailed by supra-national institutions like the IMF, WB, and the WTO.

In addition to the earlier forms of wealth extraction practised during the first and second waves, new forms emerge or old forms acquire new importance. Monopoly rents become the main form of wealth extraction. Royalties from IPRs and other income from information rents assume major significance. Because of the huge disparity in costs, trade between information economies and other economies becomes even more unequal. Compare, for instance, a CDROM which might sell for three hundred dollars, but is produced for around three dollars, to a typical Philippine product like sugar, which might sell for fifteen cents per pound. Much of the three hundred dollars in the price of 2,000 pounds of sugar would barely cover production costs, while much of the three hundred dollars in the price of a CDROM would be profit. Technology also makes possible high-speed, finely-tuned financial speculation. As the importance of the nation-state recedes and national currencies are buffeted by devaluation and other woes, corporations are able to purchase State assets and public properties at bargain prices.

New technologies of exploitation are introduced. First wave technologies were designed for the immediate plunder of our natural resources and human communities. Second wave technologies were based on material exploitation and intensive energy utilization. Third wave technologies are invariably information-based, centered on extracting the highest monopoly rents from the control of information infrastructure or information content. The best example of a technology that is at the leading edge of the third wave of globalization is the Internet. Advanced information and communications technologies make possible the convergence of media, entertainment, data, and communications. The application of information technology to genetic engineering and biotechnologies has transformed these fields into fertile areas for information monopolies, best illustrated by the patenting of life forms.

We are already starting to feel the impact of the third wave. Stronger IPR mechanisms are increasing the cost of new technologies and making access more difficult. As the global information infrastructure reaches the remotest corners of our countries, all kinds of junk culture are flooding in and cultural homogenization is reaching new levels. In the race to introduce new commercial biotechnology products and services, reckless experimentation with new life forms is leading to biological pollution from genetically-modified organisms. Their potential for damage is infinitely greater than chemical pollutants because these organisms can reproduce by themselves, mutate and evolve. Driven by the logic of profit-making and rent-seeking, genetic engineering will pose the greatest thręat to human health and survival.

Super-exploitation

The global information economy will also enable those with vast resources to concentrate wealth further into their hands. To illustrate this capacity for super-exploitation unleashed by third wave technologies: imagine a corporation which can afford to automate its international financial transactions so that its computers could do a round-the-clock, unattended scan of the global financial markets for opportunities, make decisions automatically, and conclude a financial transaction within one second or a buy-then-sell transaction pair within two seconds, and execute such transactions 24 hours a day, 365 days a year. Compare such a corporation with less capable investors who might be able to do transactions only once a minute, once per hour, or perhaps once a day. The following table shows how soon investors would be able to double their investment funds:

Table 2: Time needed to double investment funds

	Frequency of transactions			
Profit margin for every buy-then-sell transaction (%)	**Once per day**	**Once per hour**	**Once per minute**	**Once per second**
1	4.6 mos.	5.8 days	2.3 hrs.	2.3 min.
0.1	46 mos.	58 days	23 hrs.	23 min.
0.01	38 yrs.	19 mos.	9.6 days	3.9 hrs.
0.001	380 yrs.	16 yrs.	3.2 mos.	1.6 days
0.0001	3798 yrs.	158 yrs.	2.6 yrs.	16 days
0.00001	37983 yrs.	1583 yrs.	26 yrs.	5.3 mos.

Even with the thinnest margins of profit, a suitably-equipped finance firm can potentially double its investment funds within days, if not hours. Only the largest conglomerates would have the resources and connections to set up and maintain automated, round-the-clock facilities with a global reach that can conclude a transaction every second. We had better think again, those among us who dream that the Third World can leap-frog second wave economies and ride the third wave by surfing the Web or by selling our farm and factory products and our cheaper labor over the Internet. While we are still saving money to upgrade our obsolete computers, they will have multiplied their investment funds many times over.

We face a new personification of greed, one that has rid itself of distracting human feelings like love, compassion, charity, guilt, fear and other emotions, leaving only pure, unencumbered greed, free to pursue single-mindedly the one and only thing that motivates it: profit. It is the search for profit by global corporations that powers the whole process. These corporations have even acquired their own rights, which often take precedence over the rights of real persons. They have learned to nourish themselves and to grow by feeding on nature, people, and information. They have become increasingly aggressive in asserting their freedoms ("liberalization"), overcoming government controls ("deregulation") and taking over government activities ("privatization").

Corporations had earlier shared global rule with governments. Now, they want to rule it by themselves ("globalization").

The colonization of our countries that began in the 16th century hasn't really stopped. It just changed forms, coming in waves of globalization that intrude into our communities, impose their unwanted rule, and squeeze the wealth out of our people and environment. Each advance in technology, each investment of capital, creates new ways of extracting wealth from us, continually enriching those who control the technology and our economy while impoverishing us, destroying local livelihoods, ravaging our natural resources, and poisoning our environment. The first wave has ebbed, but we are still deep within the second wave, and the third wave has already started lapping our shores.

Responding to the third globalization wave

How do we respond to globalization? To the first wave, we responded with independence struggles, ranging from armed revolutions to peaceful lobbies for independence. Economically, our responses ranged from outright confiscation and nationalization of foreign property, to negotiated purchases of foreign corporations at full commercial prices. Thus, historically, we can identify a period of economic nationalism worldwide, when newly-independent countries in Asia, Africa and Latin America tried to regain control of their economies through a range of policies favoring local economic interests and institutions.

Then came the post-colonial second wave of globalization, both in response to our independence struggles and as a consequence of internal developments within the economies of powerful countries themselves. Responses to this second wave have ranged from communist-led armed struggles, to elite-led protectionist regimes. Many of these responses have floundered as crises upon crises beset our countries, enabling former colonial masters to recover much of their early privileges. In general, the second wave of globalization remains dominant over our national and community life, having managed so far to counter all the various responses that have confronted it.

We're still under the second wave, and now comes the third wave. How do we respond to this new wave, and how should our response be related to our continuing efforts to confront the second wave of globalization?

A Green response

Social movements are beginning to respond to the specific issues involving the information economy. An illustrative set of responses can be seen in the programme of the Philippine Greens for a non-monopolistic information sector (*Society, Ecology and Transformation* by the Philippine Greens, 1997).

The Greens see the information sector as very important because of its special nature: information is a social good and it can be shared freely once it is created; and since information is a non-material good, the limits to material growth do not apply to information growth. The Greens consider their approach in harmony with this nature of information.

The following are the major elements of Philippine Greens' programme for the information sector: (For details, see Chapter 28)

- The right to know
- The right to privacy
- No patenting of life forms
- The moral rights of intellectuals
- The freedom to share
- Universal access
- Compulsory licensing
- Public stations
- The best lessons of our era

These responses must also be linked with ongoing struggles against the second wave of globalization. By doing so, we can bring together the widest range of people, whose unity and joint action can bring about a political structure that can comprehensively address the challenges of globalization.

As the Philippine Greens programme indicates, one of the tasks of such struggles is to develop a non-monopolistic information sector, where intellectual activity is rewarded through non-monopolistic mechanisms which are more consistent with the social nature of information. This will involve a radical rethinking of property concepts in the information sector, reinforcing similar demands for property restructuring in the industrial and agriculture sectors.

Eventually, enough social forces must be mustered to confront squarely the powerful forces of globalization. We can expect this historic confrontation to demand from us the same kind of courage, sacrifice and heroism which the earlier anti-colonial struggles demanded from our national heroes.

Final lesson

There is one final lesson, among so many, that our own colonial past teaches us. The first Spanish colony was set up in the Philippines in 1565. Over the next three centuries, colonization would encroach on most of the archipelago, except the Muslims of Mindanao and the upland indigenous tribes. Isolated rebellions would occur but could not shake Spanish rule. In 1864, a public manifesto by a Filipino priest began a Propaganda Movement, which eventually awakened our people's anti-colonial consciousness. In 1896, a full-scale revolution broke out. By 1898, the revolution had for all intents and purposes defeated Spanish colonialism.

It took some three hundred years before we Filipinos shook off the colonial mentality that immobilized most of our people and made them vulnerable to Spanish rule. The campaign for the Filipino mind took another thirty years to win. Within three years of anti-colonial armed struggle against Spain, victory was in sight.

The struggle to unmask the colonial monster was ten to a hundred times more difficult than the struggle to bring it down.

Let us keep this lesson in mind today, when we are yet at the early stages of unmasking the monster of globalization. Let not the seeming immensity of this task cloud our vision of the future, when our communities and nations shall at last be free to chart their own destinies guided by the principles of ecology, social justice and self-determination.

20. Cyberlords: rentier class of the information sector

The information sector of an economy is that sector whose products consist principally of information goods.

Information goods are non-material goods.[1] They are most easily distinguished by the fact that they can be stored in various media and when stored in electronic media, their cost of reproduction becomes negligibly low. Some examples of information goods include software, music, video, databases, books, machine designs, genetic information, and other copyrighted or patented goods.

When the information sector of an economy becomes more dominant than either its industrial or ecology sector, then that economy has become an information economy.[2] A good example of such an economy is the U.S. economy.

Information: low reproduction cost

The basic production process in the information sector involves the use of mental workers or intellectuals to produce information goods. They are often aided in this process by additional information processing tools, at the heart of which is usually a computer. Once the first copy is created, an information

---

This paper was presented in an international workshop on "The Emerging Global Information Economy and the Response of Social Movements," held by Interdoc on November 17-20, 1996 in Silang, Cavite. The workshop was held at the same time as several other NGO conferences, in parallel with the 1996 APEC meeting in Manila. It was also published in the Human Rights Forum, *Vol. 7 No. 1 (July-Dec. 1997: pp.52-67), a semi-annual journal of the Philippine Human Rights Information Center.*

product can then be transformed for storage on various media. The most flexible form of storage is electronic media. Once stored in this form, the product becomes very easy to reproduce at very little cost. If the information is stored in digital format, then perfect reproductions of the original can be made over unlimited generations of copies.

It is the recent electronic and digital revolution which has made possible the emerging dominance of the information sector in some countries.

The ease with which information, especially in its electronic format, can now be reproduced leads to the basic conflict within the information sector. On the one hand, information users tend to share copies of information products freely. On the other hand, information producers tend to hinder the free exchange of information, so that they can maintain the extremely high profit margins possible from the negligibly low reproduction costs.

The extra-high margins of a successful information-based company are best seen in Microsoft, which grew to a billion-dollar firm within a decade after it released its first major software product. This is a feat which probably has no equal among industrial firms.

The high profit margins among information firms likewise draw finance capital from industrial and agricultural sectors. The transformation of the U.S. from an industrial to an information economy reflects this movement of investment capital towards the information sector, confirming the observation that investment capital tends to flow towards business prospects with the highest rates of return.

Monopolistic information economies

The U.S. information economy is a monopolistic information economy, because the propertied classes of the dominant information sector assert their control over information through monopolistic mechanisms called intellectual property rights (IPR).

The main forms of IPR are patents and copyrights, both of which are statutory monopolies, i.e., monopolies acquired by virtue of government statutes. These State-granted monopolies cover the exclusive rights to use, manufacture, copy, modify, and sell the product. Recently, under the GATT/WTO, these rights have been expanded further to include the exclusive right to rent and to import the products.

These statutory monopolies, which are gradually being strengthened and extended as the political and economic power of the propertied classes of the information sector grows, are in direct conflict with the information freedoms sought by the vast majority of information users. These freedoms include the freedoms to use, to share with others, and to modify information. Information monopolies are also in conflict with the basic nature of information itself as a public good.

In the future, non-monopolistic information economies may emerge, which will remunerate intellectual activity through means other than monopolistic mechanisms such as patents, copyrights, and other IPR. In such an economy, the nature of intellectual rewards will be in much better harmony with the nature of information itself.[3] This analysis covers monopolistic information economies. For convenience, the shorter term 'information economies' will be used for the rest of this article to refer to monopolistic information economies.

Classes in the information sector

Just like the ecology and industrial sectors, the information sector gives rise to various economic classes based on the individuals' position in the production, distribution and use of information. An analysis of these classes will give us useful insights about the underlying economic interests and typical attitudes of various social groups in the sector.[4] The following major classes can be identified:

Cyberlords. The cyberlords are the propertied class of the information sector. They control either a body of information, or the material infrastructure for creating, distributing or using information. Cyberlords are a rent-seeking capitalist class.[5]

The first category of cyberlords are the IPR holders, who have staked their monopoly rights over a specific body of information, and who earn their income by charging royalties, license fees, or other forms of rent from those who want to use this body of information. Cyberlords include the owners of software companies, database companies, audio, video and film companies, genetic engineering firms, pharmaceutical and seed firms, and similar companies who earn most of their income from IPR rents.

The second category of cyberlords are the infrastructure owners. They own or control the industrial infrastructure for creating, reproducing, distributing, or using information. They earn their income by charging rents for the use of these infrastructures. This category includes the owners of communication lines and equipment, radio and TV stations, Internet service providers, theater distributors and owners, cable TV operators, and other firms through which information controlled by the first category is reproduced, distributed, or used. Strictly speaking, these infrastructure owners are an industrial rather than an information class, but are doubly-classed as cyberlords because they are a rent-seeking class who play a key role in the distribution of information.

However, these industrial cyberlords may not share the same rabid advocacy for IPRs that characterize the IPR-holding cyberlords, especially when IPRs impede the wider use of the infrastructure from which they derive their own income. This category is generally in alliance with the first; nonetheless, the distinction between them may become important occasionally, in the struggle against the cyberlords of the first type, who are the true cyberlords of the information economy.[6]

We can also include in the cyberlord class those highly-paid professionals who earn their living under the employ or in the service of cyberlords. The best examples are the top-level managers as well as the lawyers who serve cyberlords and who derive their income mostly from payments by the cyberlords they work for. Lawyers, in particular, are absolutely necessary for copyrights and patents holders because these IPR instruments are basically legal artifices which can only be implemented through government action. These highly-paid hirelings acquire the class status and the ideological outlook of the cyberlords they serve.

Information cyberlords can be classified into big cyberlords, middle cyberlords and small cyberlords.

The big cyberlords earn most of their income from information rents. The mark of the big cyberlord stratum is that it did not create some or even most of the body of information protected by its patents or copyrights. They were instead created by hired staff, contracted out or bought from other companies. Big cyberlords normally start out as small or middle cyberlords. As they acquire economic power, they find it more convenient to pay others for existing information products than to create new ones themselves from scratch. When they do so, they turn into big cyberlords. Big cyberlords often buy into or buy out smaller cyberlords not only to acquire new products but also to suppress potential or actual competition. The best example of a big cyberlord is William Gates, the principal owner of Microsoft and the richest person in the world.

Big cyberlords all over the world are scouring the public domain for information products that they can privatize and monopolize through IPRs. Some have already acquired the exclusive electronic reproduction rights to the paintings and other cultural artifacts in the world's best museums. Others are engaged in a race to patent genetic information of all kinds, including parts of the human genome. Still others are turning their eye on the vast information outputs of governments, which are normally in the public domain.

Like Microsoft, most corporations owned by big cyberlords operate globally. These firms comprise a big portion of the hidden forces driving the process of globalization. Because the social nature of information keeps asserting itself and information products tend to spread themselves globally as soon as they are released, cyberlords need a global legal infrastructure for imposing their information monopolies and extracting monopoly rents. Thus, they push the globalization process incessantly to ensure that every country, every nook and corner of the globe, is within the reach of their mechanisms for extracting monopoly rents.[7]

The biggest information cyberlords are based mostly in the U.S., Europe, and, to a lesser extent, Japan. In these countries, the highly-advanced industrial infrastructure, together with extremist concepts of private property, have given their cyberlord class a huge, commanding lead over cyberlords elsewhere.[8] Their presence is felt globally, and because they tend to suppress local efforts to acquire new technologies at the least cost, big cyberlords are a major hindrance to the development efforts of most national economies.

Like the big cyberlords, middle cyberlords earn most of their income from information rents. However, the incomes of middle cyberlords come principally from the rent income generated by the body of information much of which they created themselves. Successful authors, inventors, and songwriters, who live off the royalties from their works, belong to this category.

Small cyberlords earn substantial income from information rents, but their income is not sufficient to support themselves and their family, so they have to supplement it with incomes from other sources. Most local information cyberlords belong to this category.

This stratum keeps trying to graduate to the middle cyberlord status, because they have internalized the ideology of the cyberlord class. This ideology arises from the basic dream of the cyberlord class, which can be summed up as follows: "create a good idea or 'expression of an idea,' stake a monopoly claim over it through a patent or a copyright, and then live off the rents for the rest of your life." Small cyberlords are in perpetual pursuit of this dream, and a few may manage to become middle cyberlords.

Compradors. They are the merchant capitalists of the information sector. They earn their living by selling for profit patented or copyrighted products. They very often come from the merchant classes of the industrial and ecology sectors, and may retain their businesses in these sectors. These merchant classes are attracted to move into the information sector because the extremely high profit margins enjoyed by successful cyberlords gives resellers better margins too.

This class can be roughly divided into two. Monopolistic compradors make money by paying cyberlords for the right to sell patented or copyrighted goods. Thus, they derive their income from information rents and are therefore supportive of cyberlord interests.

Non-monopolistic compradors make money by reproducing and selling patented or copyrighted material, without paying the monopoly rents claimed by cyberlords. In a way, they help break the information monopolies imposed by cyberlords.

Because of the political clout of cyberlords, the non-monopolistic compradors are often harassed and suppressed, to discourage them from their trade and to turn them into monopolistic compradors. They are frequently the targets of surveillance, legal suits, raids, and other forms of government and cyberlord harassment. Yet, there is no lack of non-monopolistic compradors who trade in copyrighted and patented materials, making these materials more accessible to the public which would otherwise be unable to afford them. Even under the worst forms of authoritarian rule, non-monopolistic compradors will continue to ply their trade by forming an underground network to break the cyberlord monopolies. These compradors can be allies of information users against the cyberlord class. Many of them, however, eventually surrender to the power of cyberlords, arrive at a profit-sharing arrangement with them, and turn into monopolistic compradors.

Intellectuals. Intellectuals are the main creators of information in the information sector. They earn their living through mental labor, creating new and useful information. The intellectual class may be further subdivided into three strata.

The upper stratum earns some income from information rents but this is not substantial. Most of their earnings are from business contracts for information work, rather than IPR rents. This stratum will often defend IPRs because its members already derive income from information rents and hope to get more income from such rents in the future.

The upper stratum's rent income from IPR distinguishes it from the middle stratum, which has no such rent income.

The middle stratum gets its income from business contracts for information work. Some members of this stratum may retain their fixed-wage jobs, although the bigger portion of their income already comes from their contractual work. This can be common especially among intellectuals in government.

This stratum earns no income from information rents. However, members of this stratum sometimes successfully negotiate to retain ownership over their work, to prevent the other contracting party from commercializing it. This represents an incipient cyberlord thinking that is strengthened or suppressed depending on their success or failure in retaining full ownership over their work in these negotiations and in extracting rent income from their body of work. In the main, however, this stratum does not closely identify with the interests of monopolistic cyberlords.

The middle stratum differs from the lower stratum in that it is profit-making rather than wage-earning, and that members of this stratum may have other intellectuals under their employ.

The lower stratum consists of the wage-earning intellectuals, who earn most of their income from fixed-rate payments such as wages and salaries. They may occasionally get additional remunerations such as bonuses for especially useful intellectual work, or side contracts from which they may earn considerable sums. But they earn the bulk of their income as wage-earners.

Should their work result in patentable or copyrightable materials, their hiring contracts normally specify that such materials become the property of the company they work for. Because they are usually in no position to negotiate when looking for a job, they accept such contracts as a matter of course. The majority of intellectuals belong to this stratum of the intellectual class.

Information users. Members of this group use information but are not generally involved in the creation of information products. Whatever information they generate are either automatically shared with others, or kept confidential. The idea of staking a monopoly on a body of information so that they can make money out of it is quite alien to this group. Because they generally earn their income from elsewhere, information users are actually not a single class nor a monolithic group, but a cluster of classes in the ecology, industrial and information sectors. In so far as they are all information users, however, they actively seek the information freedoms of using, sharing, and modifying information. Information users are therefore the main force in the struggle to free information from cyberlord monopolies.

The basic conflict

The key issue that separates classes in a monopolistic information economy is the issue of IPR, which reflects their class roles in the production, distribution and use of information. IPRs are a highly monopolistic form of controlling information flow, and are therefore totally incompatible with the nature of information as well as the desire of information users to use, share and modify information freely.

Cyberlords are very strong advocates for expanding these monopoly rights, while information users want to limit these rights as much as possible. In so far as IPR infringements impinge on their profit margins, compradors will take the side of cyberlords. But in so far as monopoly rents themselves impinge on their profit margins, other compradors will oppose IPRs. Intellectuals may dream of owning in the future a body of information from which they can themselves extract information rents. In the main, however, they realize that this cannot be their main source of income, and that they themselves need access to many bodies of information which are currently monopolized through patents or copyrights.

The key to the transformation of a monopolistic information economy towards a non-monopolistic information economy is to replace monopolistic IPRs with other means of rewarding intellectual activity. This transformation will of course be opposed to the very end by the cyberlord class, which furthermore is politically and economically very strong. As the privatization process subsumes under cyberlord monopolies more and more of what is now public domain information, the public of information users will acquire a higher level of political consciousness, and this struggle will eventually express itself as the main conflict in a monopolistic information economy. As such, it will increasingly manifest itself in cultural, economic as well as political fronts.

A class strategy against monopolies

The class strategy that can defeat the powerful cyberlord class, involves advancing a set of demands that will isolate the big cyberlords and their closest comprador allies, neutralize or win over the middle and small cyberlords, and win over and mobilize the entire intellectual class with special attention to its middle and lower strata, to unite with the vast majority of information users. This united front should also involve other classes and social groups in the industrial and ecology sectors who are themselves information users or whose thinking and orientation are in conflict with some aspects of IPRs. The latter group include indigenous peoples, farmers, women, and the religious sector. Without such a united front, it will be extremely difficult to defeat the information monopolies of the big cyberlords, and the latter would be able to use their increasing economic and political power to consolidate, codify and further expand their statutory monopolies.

With a well-formulated set of demands, the powerful cyberlord class can be politically isolated, and existing laws can be restructured to liberalize access to monopolistically-owned information. The long-term goal is to dismantle monopolistic forms of information ownership and to replace them with non-monopolistic forms which are more in harmony with the nature of information itself. This will eventually enable users to enjoy the full information freedoms that will unleash creativity not only among the intellectuals but among information users themselves.

The formulation of such a comprehensive set of demands, which in effect becomes the basis of political strategy and tactics in the emerging class conflicts within the information sector, deserves a separate piece. However, several demands can be identified now, because they have emerged historically and must become part of the overall set of demands against information monopolies.

Compulsory licensing. The most important demand for breaking the information monopolies of cyberlords is the retention of compulsory licensing and the expansion of its coverage.

Compulsory licensing works as follows: Somebody who wants to use/commercialize patented or copyrighted material approaches *not* the patent or copyright holder, but the government for a license to do so. The government grants the license, whether the original patent or copyright holder agrees or not, but compels the licensee to pay the patent/copyright holder a royalty rate that is fixed by the government (or by law). Many countries in the world have used and continue to use compulsory licensing for important products like pharmaceuticals and books.[9]

Compulsory licensing (also called mandatory licensing in some countries) is a demand of many countries who want to access technologies but cannot afford the price set by patent/copyright holders. While this internationally-recognized mechanism was meant for the benefit of poorer countries, even the U.S. and many European countries use it.

Most small cyberlords, because they often have neither the capital nor the production facilities to commercialize their creations themselves, welcome compulsory licensing, although they will try to negotiate for higher royalty rates. They welcome it because compulsory licensing will ensure them some income from their creations. Compulsory licensing is the demand that can split the cyberlord class and win over or neutralize the small cyberlords and some of the middle cyberlords. The big cyberlords, who have the capability to commercialize products themselves, are violently opposed to the idea of compulsory licensing because it is a powerful threat to their monopoly over information. It is an indication of the political power and influence of cyberlords that they managed to thoroughly emasculate the concept of compulsory licensing in the GATT/WTO agreement.

Non-monopolistic compradors welcome compulsory licensing because it legalizes their anti-monopolistic trading activities, protecting them from legal harassments, raids, and other attacks initiated by big cyberlords.

No patenting of life forms. This demand emerged out of the popular campaigns against genetic engineering and recombinant DNA technologies. It has become a major global issue, as biotechnology in general and genetic engineering in particular continue to take that slippery slope leading corporations towards the direct manipulation and commercialization of human genetic material. True to their cyberlord nature, owners of biotech firms are racing against each other in patenting DNA sequences, microorganisms, plants, animals, human genetic matter and all other kinds of biological material. Cyberlord representatives have already managed to insert in the GATT/WTO agreement protection for patents on microorganisms and microbiological processes.

This is a very powerful demand because biotech cyberlords impinge on religious and moral issues as well as on indigenous community knowledge. Genetic engineering also threatens to give rise to a whole new class of harmful viruses, germs, microorganisms and higher life forms which have no natural enemies. This demand can unite a wide range of sectors against the cyberlord ideology.

Expanding the fair-use policy. This has been the historical struggle waged by librarians, particularly of public libraries, who see themselves as guardians of the world's storehouse of knowledge. Most librarians want to see this storehouse of knowledge freely accessible to the public, and they have fought long battles and firmly held their ground on the issue of "fair-use," which allows students and researchers access to copyrighted or patented materials without paying IPR rents. Recently, this ground has been suffering from slow erosion due to the increasing political power of cyberlords. The expansion of the fair-use policy can be a minor victory against the overwhelming advances of cyberlords in various fronts to expand the scope and coverage of their monopolies.

Support for non-monopolistic mechanisms. Various concepts in software development and/or distribution have recently emerged. Some, such as shareware, are less monopolistic than IPR. Others, such as "copyleft" and the GNU General Public License (GPL), are completely non-monopolistic.

Shareware works under various schemes, such as free trial periods, free distribution, voluntary payments, etc. These concepts have in effect abandoned the legal artifice of asserting one's exclusive monopoly over copying one's work, in favor of granting users limited rights to use, copy and distribute the material. While shareware authors have shed considerably the monopolistic ideology of cyberlords, they still balk at releasing their source code, and therefore continue to keep their users captive and unable to modify the software on their own.

The GNU GPL enables users to enjoy the fullest set of information freedoms, including the freedom to use, the freedom to share with others, and the freedom to modify information. The GPL shows how current copyright concepts may be used in the transition away from monopolistic arrangements, and points the way towards future non-monopolistic software development.[10] Software as well as books which fall under the GPL copyright may be used freely by anybody who may find them useful. They may also be shared freely with others. Finally, the software may be freely modified because the source code is included in the distribution.

Software source code is the equivalent of architectural plans in case of buildings, schematic diagrams in case of electronic equipment, or technical drawings in case of machinery. To improve software, a building, electronic equipment, or machinery, you must have these original plans to do the modifications properly. Otherwise, the original plans must be reconstructed before major modifications can proceed.

The extremes which cyberlords resort to, in order to strengthen their monopolies, can be seen from their persistent and increasingly successful demand that countries outlaw the decompilation of software.[11] Decompilation is the reconstruction of software source code. It is equivalent to reconstructing architectural plans, schematic diagrams, or technical drawings, because the original designers refused to release them to the user. By prohibiting the reconstruction of these original plans, cyberlords make it extremely difficult if not impossible for users to independently modify copyrighted or patented materials, denying users their freedom to modify the materials and enabling cyberlords to extract even more monopoly rents from users.

General wage increases. In a way, salaries and wages are a specific form of non-monopolistic remuneration for intellectual activity. This is the most relevant demand for the big majority of intellectuals, who will stay on the side of information users as long as they are assured of some reasonable remuneration for their work as information creators. In this respect, the big majority of intellectuals can unite with other wage-earning classes to raise common demands.

The list above is not complete. A comprehensive set of demands for transforming monopolistic information economies can only emerge when the various classes ranged against the cyberlords acquire an economic and political consciousness that will make clear-cut where their interests lie.[12]

Towards a new social order

These demands in the information sector must also be linked with the demands of other change-oriented classes and groups in the ecology and industrial sectors, such as farmers, fisherfolk, workers, women and indigenous peoples. The key is to bring together the widest range of people, whose unity and joint action can bring about a political structure for evolving new forms of rewarding intellectual activity. Such forms will lead in the future to a non-monopolistic information sector. The rethinking of property concepts that this will bring about will then reinforce demands for restructuring the industrial and agriculture sectors as well.

From such a confluence of social movements, enough social forces for change can emerge to bring forth a society where knowledge and culture are freely shared, where industrial machinery are carefully designed for genuine human and community needs, and where agriculture is an ecological and not an industrial undertaking.

Notes:

[1] Information goods. Information, in the most general sense, is anything that can be represented and stored as a digital series of bits (i.e., one's and zero's). In the information sciences, information is defined in terms of resolving uncertainty about a set of possible outcomes. To acquire information means to reduce or to completely resolve the uncertainty. This clearly makes information a non-material entity.

[2] Information, industrial, and ecology sectors. I am referring here to the sectors of the economy that engage in the production of goods. I use the ecology sector to cover both agriculture and hunting/gathering. Fishing, for example, is a hunting/gathering activity, which is part of the ecology sector. A more complete set of economic sectors would include the personal and the financial services sectors (both of which involve services more than goods).

[3] Non-monopolistic forms of remuneration. These include salaries and wages, bonuses, prizes, awards, grants and other means of remunerating intellectual activity which don't give intellectuals the exclusive right to use or copy their creation.

[4] Class analysis. It is sometimes considered unfair to lump individual cyberlords into a single class, as if these people had no conscience, moral values, or social ethics. It is true that some individuals, perhaps due to personal belief, religion, or political inclination, may act against their own economic interests. If they do so consistently, however, they probably will not remain a cyberlord for long. Also, most of the big and middle cyberlords run their business affairs through corporations. Obviously, corporations have neither heart, conscience nor soul. These are invariably run by managers whose pay and job security depend on how well they maximize corporate profits. Thus, it remains valid to look at the economic interests of classes, to acquire some useful insights into their members' most probable economic, political and social behavior.

[5] Cyberlord. The word is constructed from "cyberspace" and "landlord." The information space created by all the storage and transmission media connected to the Internet is often called cyberspace. Landlords, i.e., landowners who charge rent for the use of their land, are the classical example of a rent-seeking class.

[6] Conflict of interest between industrial and information cyberlords. For instance, a lot of commercial software are freely exchanged among on-line users. On-line providers like CompuServe or America Online either turn a blind eye on these activities or claim that they are impossible to police. Since most on-line providers charge their subscribers per minute of usage, it is also obvious that the more such exchanges occur, the more money they make.

[7] Globalization. The Internet, the international media, the continuing pressure on countries to open up their economies to global corporations, and the GATT/WTO are examples of mechanisms that facilitate the globalization process.

[8] Extremist private property concepts. One example is the claim of scientists that if they discover a particular human DNA sequence, they can claim ownership over this sequence through a patent. This means that they will have the exclusive right to use, copy, commercialize, rent out, import, etc. such DNA sequence. Another example is the claim of scientists, who splice a strand of DNA from one life form to another, that they have created a new life form, and thus can patent it. Such a patent is an ownership claim not only on the particular result of such a genetic experiment, but on all subsequent life deriving from it, such as its offsprings and descendants. Still another example is the ownership by some companies of the exclusive electronic reproduction rights to some of the world's most famous art works. Such ownership means that they, alone, can reproduce electronically these art works.

[9] In the Philippines, we have a Book Reprinting Law, which authorizes local publishers to reprint foreign textbooks for the use of the local educational system. Philippine law also provides for compulsory licensing by local companies of pharmaceutical products. Both laws are currently under heavy attack by cyberlord lobbyists.

[10] GNU GPL. GNU is a project of the Free Software Foundation (FSF), under the leadership of Richard Stallman. Its General Public License (GPL) was carefully crafted to make use of existing copyright concepts to pave the way for a non-monopolistic form of copyright. The increasing popularity among Unix users of the Linux kernel by Linus Torvalds, the GNU operating system of the FSF, and free alternatives to MS-DOS and Windows – all distributed under the GPL – shows the way for future non-monopolistic software development. Check the Web page http://www.gnu.ai.mit.edu/philosophy/categories.html for details about the GNU GPL.

[11] Decompilation. The Business Software Alliance (BSA), which represents the interests of cyberlords worldwide, has launched an aggressive lobby within the Philippine legislature to ban decompilation.

[12] An effort to formulate the response of social movements to the emerging information economy was made by Interdoc, an international network of non-government organizations, in a workshop last November 1996 in Silang, Cavite, Philippines. One formulation which emerged from the workshop is as follows: "Build, improve and expand the body of public domain information infrastructures, tools and content."

21. Testing the political strength of a cyberlord

The legal action brought by the U.S. Justice Department and 20 American states against Microsoft Corporation for monopolistic practices is not an ordinary anti-monopoly case.

It is also a major test of political strength for the leading member of the cyberlord class, the emerging elite class of the global information economy.

A rent-seeking class

Like landlords, cyberlords are a rent-seeking class. They make money by acquiring exclusive control over a resource and charging rents for its use. Microsoft, for example, earns its income from a form of rent called royalty, which is what you pay when you get yourself an official copy of its software products. If you sign the copyright agreement that comes with the product, you have in fact acknowledged a monopoly by agreeing that your payment did not buy you anything except permission from Microsoft to use their software.

There is no doubt about the monopoly status of Microsoft in the information sector, not only in the U.S. or here in the Philippines but throughout the world.

Its MS-Windows (versions 3.x, 95 and NT) together with the older MS-DOS control more than 90% of the operating system market for personal computers. Microsoft also controls more than three-quarters of the software applications market (word processors, spreadsheets, presentation software, and database managers), and

---

A version of this piece appeared in the column "Second Opinion" in the daily newspaper, Philippine Journal, *on October 23, 1998.*

more than half of the software development tools market of language interpreters and compilers (Visual Basic, Visual C and C++, etc.).

In areas where it is not yet the dominant vendor, Microsoft is usually just behind the leader and coming up steadily, using as leverage its dominance in operating systems, development tools, and applications.

Monopolistic practices

The case against Microsoft, however, is not just about its monopoly status. It is also about the company's monopolistic – others have used the term "predatory" – practices in order to attain that status.

Among the monopolistic practices that Microsoft has used are the following (my thanks to NetAction's Nathan Newman of San Francisco, California for much of the data):

- *Giving away products to kill competition*: Small and innovative companies used to thrive around Microsoft's operating systems by offering useful software utilities for such tasks as unfragmenting disks, compressing data, removing viruses, etc. Microsoft would develop a similar program or buy one on the market and then distribute it free with its operating systems, killing the smaller companies. The latest example of this anti-competitive practice is Microsoft's effort to include with every copy of its Windows software a free Internet browser that competes directly with Netscape's Navigator.

Using its dominant position in one area to solidify its position in another area: Microsoft's break into the operating system (OS) market came when computer giant IBM chose it to provide the OS for the IBM PC, the computer which eventually became the dominant desktop standard in the market. The OS is the link between the computer hardware and the application programs, all of which depend on the OS to operate properly. A slight change in the OS can suddenly make a perfectly-working application behave erratically, damaging its market credibility. Microsoft's control over the PC OS gave Microsoft products a huge edge over competitors. Early Windows versions, for example, issued false error messages which gave the impression that DR-DOS, an MS-DOS competitor, was not compatible with Windows. A late Windows version, on the other hand, was called an "OS/2 killer" because the minor changes it introduced caused compatibility problems with a major competitor, IBM's OS/2. Both DR-DOS and OS/2 were generally considered better products than their Microsoft counterparts.

Buying out small and promising competitors who sell better products: Microsoft has a long history of buying out or buying into competitors and other companies. Through its purchases, Microsoft douses competition, strengthens its market share and establishes dominance in an area. Here's a partial list: online news (MSNBC, $500M); Internet access device (Web TV Networks, $425M); 3D animation (Softimage, $177M); database management (Fox software, $175M); computer systems (Apple, $150M stake); Web site management (Vermeer, $80-130M); disk compression (Stacker, $40M); speech recognition (Lernout & Hauspie, $45M); server software (SCO Unix, 11.5%); voice recognition (Wildfire); web tools (Aspect Engineering); video streaming technology (VDONet, 5% and Vxtreme, $75M); electronic mailboxes (Hotmail); Internet infrastructure (UUNet, 13%); customized business news (iNews, 7.4%); translation facilities (Translators Workbench, 20%).

Pressuring hardware vendors to sell only Microsoft products: To kill DR-DOS, for example, an emerging competitor to MS-DOS in the late 1980's, Microsoft required hardware manufacturers and resellers to pay Microsoft a license fee for every machine they sold, whether this machine included MS-DOS or another operating system like DR-DOS. Japanese officials actually raided the Microsoft office in Tokyo, because it was suspected of requiring Japanese PC makers to offer Microsoft applications, to the exclusion of a competing Japanese company.

Entering into a market-sharing agreement with competitors: This is the U.S. Justice Department's charge against Microsoft, that it tried in 1995 to convince its competitor Netscape to carve up the browser market.

Expanding its reach

As a result of these and other anti-competitive practices, Microsoft has not only solidified its monopolistic status in the fields it dominates; the company is also now positioned to expand its reach into new areas such as financial software, electronic banking, servers, network operating systems, Internet software (browsers, Web servers, development tools). Beyond software, it is also expanding into entertainment, training, financial transactions, and electronic commerce

To break up monopolies such as Microsoft's, the best option for the Philippines is compulsory licensing, an internationally-recognized mechanism against monopolies.

Can U.S. justice defeat the top cyberlord?

Despite the very strong case against the Microsoft monopoly, it remains to be seen whether the U.S. Justice Department will win its case against the software giant.

Cyberlords like Microsoft Chairman Bill Gates have been gradually acquiring political clout, reflecting the increasing economic dominance of the information sector in the U.S. economy. The voice of the cyberlord class is already dominant in U.S. diplomacy and trade negotiations. The top concern of cyberlords, the protection of their intellectual property rights, is now the number one U.S. demand – and a non-negotiable one – in bilateral as well as multilateral trade negotiations. They also have in Al Gore – today the U.S. vice-president and tomorrow, who knows? – a powerful ally if not spokesman for their interests. But their political influence is only now beginning to permeate into much of the Washington bureaucracy. The anti-trust action against Microsoft comes at a time when the cyberlord class has not fully established its political dominance as much as its economic dominance.

If Microsoft wins its case, then we'll know that the new elite class of the information economy has finally entrenched itself politically too.

22. Globalization: poor design?

Most successful designers of complex systems follow basic rules of design.

Whether it is a spaceship that will land men on the moon, or a worldwide network of ten million computers such as the Internet, or a huge computer program with fifty million lines of code, or a tiny computer chip with two million transistors on it, the design rules are surprisingly similar.

One of the most basic rules in designing complex systems is called modularization. The rule says one should break up a complex system into smaller parts. These smaller parts – usually called modules – should be more manageable and relatively independent from each other. The modules should interact only through a few well-defined interfaces. Each module should have high internal cohesion. The coupling between modules should be minimized.

A good example is the Apollo lunar mission. One of the most complex systems ever made by human beings, it used modularization all throughout, from the design of the spaceship itself, to the electronic circuitry that comprised much of its automatic intelligence. The mission's spectacular success is a tribute to the effectiveness of modular design.

Another example is the Internet, a computer network designed to survive a nuclear attack. Again, the basic rule in the design of the Internet was modularization. The Internet implements communications through relatively independent network layers which interact with each other only through well-defined interfaces. Internet communications protocols have also been broken down

---

This piece was published by the Philippine News and Features (PNF) in August 1996, before the 1997 Asian financial crisis.

into simpler protocols. There is a protocol for transferring mail, another for news, and still another for files.

In economics, modularization means that countries should try to become as self-sufficient as possible and as independent from each other as possible. It means that interaction between economies should be minimized and should occur only through well-defined regulations. Coupling among economies should be minimal.

Globalization, the current trend among economic planners, violates the design principle of modularization. By tearing down "well-defined interfaces" between economies, globalization increases the coupling among countries and makes countries more instead of less dependent on each other.

A complex system with high interaction among its parts becomes more prone to system failures. It is difficult to modify and to improve. It becomes error-prone, yet the errors are more difficult to identify and to correct. In a poorly-designed system, attempts to correct errors often introduce more errors into the system, making it even more failure-prone.

From a systems view, a globalized economy is a badly designed economy. It will be prone to errors and failures. It will be difficult to maintain and to improve. Attempts at correcting its failures will result in even worse problems.

Look at the problems of today's globalized economy. Because of the free movement of goods, diseases spread quickly from one corner of the globe to another. CFCs produced in one country damage the ozone layer and threaten the health of the citizens of other countries. Toxic wastes produced in the North find themselves being dumped in the South. Chernobyl's radioactive emissions threatened the dairy industry of the rest of Europe. A stock market crash in the U.S. would probably send stock prices worldwide tumbling. Because of the free movement of capital, job insecurity as well as speculation has become a global problem.

These are all the consequences of the bad design inherent in a tightly coupled global economy.

Despite this, economists often insist that globalization is inevitable, and the best we can do is to adjust to it.

For a designer's viewpoint, of course, there is no such thing as "inevitable." Every design is the result of a conscious or unconscious effort. Poor designs become inevitable only because the designer relaxes on his rules, and adopts an "anything goes" approach. To the economist, on the other hand, relaxing the rules is called "liberalization," "deregulation," or "leveling the playing field." And "anything goes" is called "free-market competition." A relaxation of the rules then makes it easy to violate the basic principles of good design, and makes globalization inevitable.

Who want the rules relaxed? Mostly the global corporations, the main beneficiaries of globalization. They are the equivalent of global variables in software.

Software engineers try to eliminate global variables or turn them into local variables. Because global variables can easily cause changes behind the back of the system designer, they make the whole system unreliable and crash-prone. When global corporations use transfer pricing to maximize profits at the expense of the host country, or when they switch to highly automated equipment and minimize local employment, or when they compete with local entrepreneurs for skilled labor or for bank loans, or when they suddenly pull out liquid assets for some reason or another, we are witnessing what system designers call the "undesirable side-effects of global variables." Thus a fundamental rule in system design is to avoid global variables.

Faced with a badly-designed, non-modular system, designers frequently find it easier and more cost-effective to simply junk the design and to start from scratch.

Perhaps, this is what we should do with globalization.

23. What could be more important than efficiency? (A critique of efficiency as the main criterion for economic decision-making)

In an earlier letter to the *Human Ecology Review*[2], I proposed reliability as an alternative criterion for socio-economic decision-making instead of efficiency. This paper pursues that idea further.

Definitions

Efficiency is a measure of how well transformation of matter or energy occurs. To be efficient means to get the most from the least. The higher the efficiency, the better the transformation is occurring. Efficiency is usually computed from the ratio of useful output to input. To be accurate, the computation must take into account all inputs to a process; otherwise, the computed efficiency may exceed 100%. This will imply that the transformation process itself is creating new matter or energy, which contradicts fundamental laws of physics.

Since energy transformation always produces waste heat, the energy efficiency of any process is always less than 100%. If some of the material outputs are not usable (e.g., wastes), then the sum of the useful material outputs will be less than the sum of the material inputs too, and the material efficiency of the process will likewise be less than 100%.

This piece was circulated by the author in 2001.

[2] *Verzola, Roberto, "Industry, Efficiency and Corporations,"* Human Ecology Review, *Vol. 6 No. 2, 1999:p.121.*

Economists often express the inputs and outputs of a process in monetary terms, because their interest is in processes where the monetary outputs exceed the monetary inputs. Furthermore, economists often compute the difference instead of ratio between outputs and inputs, because their interest is in absolute monetary amounts instead of ratios. In such cases where the focus is on absolute amounts, this paper uses the term "gain" instead of "efficiency." An example of gain is the producer's profit, which is revenues minus costs. Another example is the total utility to the consumer of a set of goods minus the total price of these goods.

Because both are measures of output relative to input, gain is closely related to efficiency and is used whenever absolute magnitudes are more important than relative magnitudes. Among business firms, gain is really of more interest than efficiency, the best firms being those who manage to squeeze the last marginal bit of gain (i.e., profit) from their business operations. Among natural persons, the output of interest is not necessarily matter, energy, or money but a vaguer concept like welfare, utility, or happiness, which makes measuring efficiency or maximizing it harder.

Like firms, economies today also tend to maximize gain (i.e., efficiency and inputs), not only efficiency. To maximize gain, one can increase the inputs to a process, or the efficiency by which the inputs are transformed into outputs, or both. Expanding one's global reach is one way of increasing inputs. The economies-of-scale argument (higher efficiency through larger scale of operations) also supports a global strategy. Thus, gain-maximization strategies directly lead to globalization.

In practice the efficiency of an entire economy is very difficult to maximize or even to measure. To solve this problem, economists use a curious rule for improving the theoretical efficiency of economies step by step: improve somebody's welfare without reducing anybody else's, and keep doing this until nobody's welfare can be improved further without reducing somebody else's. This is the economist's Pareto efficiency, which is obviously lower than full theoretical efficiency, but is itself a theoretical construct that is hardly ever seen – not even approximated – in reality.

Efficiency and economic theory

Despite these theoretical problems, efficiency is probably the most common criterion for economic decision-making in modern society. Nearly all modern economic policies cite it as their ultimate goal, even if measuring it can be difficult.

Efficiency is the rationale for competition in a free market. It is also the reason cited for dismantling the welfare State. It is used to justify privatization programs. Advocates of the international division of labor and economies of scale cite efficiency as their goal. Globalization, which extends the economies-of-scale idea to its utmost, also invokes efficiency. When policy-makers select between alternatives, efficiency is often at the top of the list of criteria for selection.

Critiques of efficiency

The efficiency criterion has been criticized from at least three vantage points: 1) from efficiency advocates themselves; 2) from the social justice viewpoint; and 3) from the ecological viewpoint.

The first critique comes from within the advocates of efficiency itself. This critique retains efficiency as its main criterion for policy formulation, but points out flaws in the way efficiency is computed and efficiency estimates distorted, usually due to the incomplete accounting of inputs and outputs. Incomplete accounting occurs when one ignores non-market transactions or externalizes costs.

An example of non-market transactions is subsistence production, where a considerable portion of the output is for direct consumption. Unless such production is accounted for, a subsistence economy may appear an inefficient, low-output economy. In fact, production for consumption is quite efficient because it saves marketing, storage and distribution costs. An important subset of production for direct consumption is household work, the non-accounting of which is a major critique of women's movements against current economic systems.

Still another example of incomplete accounting occurs in U.S. agriculture, which prides itself in its increasing "efficiency," with less than 10% of its population producing food for twice its population size. Yet, the energetic efficiency of U.S. agriculture has actually gone down over the decades: at the start of this century, it required less than one calorie input to produce a calorie of food; today, it needs more than 10 calories to produce the same amount.

Costs are externalized by passing them on to politically-weak social sectors, to the environment, or to future generations. This can lead to false impressions of high efficiency and mask gross inefficiencies within the system.

All such types of incomplete accounting distort efficiency comparisons.

The social justice critique

The social justice critique of the efficiency criterion suggests as a higher criterion the concept of equity. According to this critique, efficiency does not ensure equitable sharing of the output and often results in a reduction in equity (i.e., increasing the gap between rich and poor).

This critique often presents efficiency as a problem of production (how to allocate input resources to maximize output), and equity as a problem of distribution (how to allocate the output to minimize the gap between rich and poor). Thus, from the vantage point of many equity critics of efficiency, maximizing efficiency and ensuring equitability are parallel objectives which may or may not conflict.

The ecological sustainability critique

The third critique of efficiency comes from the vantage point of ecology. According to this critique, efficiency only looks at a linear process that transforms input A into output B. This critique points out the problem of a linear process: the continuous transformation of input A into output B will gradually use up A and accumulate B. How will A be replaced? Where will B go? The more efficient such a linear process becomes, the faster A is used up, the faster B accumulates in the ecosystem. In a real world, a linear process is eventually an unsustainable process.

Just as the social justice critique insists that the output B must be equitably distributed, the ecological sustainability critique insists that the linear process must be turned into a cyclical one, so that the final output of the process eventually goes back to become fresh input into another – or even the same – process. This is what Barry Commoner called "closing the circle."

A new critique of the efficiency criterion

This paper proposes a fourth critique of the efficiency criterion, from the vantage point of engineering and systems design. Such a vantage point is becoming increasingly useful, since economic systems today are as much a product of social engineering and conscious design as they are a product of unplanned evolutionary development. This new critique also complements the social justice and ecological sustainability critiques of efficiency.

In engineering and systems design, another criterion for design optimization is often deemed more important than efficiency. This is the criterion of reliability.

While efficiency and reliability are related, they are not the same. Efficiency is a measure of how well a system transforms its inputs into useful output. It is usually expressed in terms of the ratio of useful output to input. Reliability is a measure of how long a system performs without failing. It is usually expressed in terms of a mean time between failures (MTBF). It may also be expressed in terms of the probability of non-failure. Reliability is closely related to risk, which is usually defined as the probability of failure multiplied by the estimated cost of the failure.

Reliability and failure

There are many ways of defining socio-economic failure. Even an extremely affluent society like the U.S. shows many signs of failure. Homelessness, unemployment, imprisonment, broken families, and poverty are examples of the failure of the U.S. system. For those who want a single measure of economic failure, below-subsistence income is one possible candidate.

Given a system's output over time, one would average the output, and divide it by the average input over a period of time to get the system's average efficiency. System failure can be defined as an instance when output goes below a minimum threshold value. To determine reliability, one would then note all instances of failure and take the mean (average) time between failures (MTBF).[3]

Note that efficiency highlights the gain in output, while reliability highlights the risk of failure. While the two are related, they are not the same. High efficiency can be achieved under unreliable conditions, and high reliability can be achieved under inefficient conditions.

For instance, a system that experiences frequent failures of extremely short duration can have low reliability without significantly reducing its efficiency. As the duration of each failure approaches zero, the reduction in efficiency becomes negligible. Such a system is highly efficient but very unreliable. Another system can have a much lower output than the first example but if it seldom fails, then it is a highly reliable but very inefficient system.

---

[3] The probability of non-failure (i.e., success) over a particular time period t may then be computed as $e^{(-t/MTBF)}$

In this paper, a strategy that improves on efficiency as well as the amount of input will be called a gain-improving strategy, while one that improves on reliability and the cost of failure will be called a risk-reducing strategy. Where the computational capabilities of economic agents allow it, these strategies may evolve into gain-maximizing and risk-minimizing strategies, respectively.

When efficiency and reliability conflict

In the engineering and design sciences, efficiency and reliability are two design considerations which often conflict, because reliability can usually be improved (e.g., through modularization or through redundancy) at the expense of efficiency. Reliability is often seen as equally important, and in many cases the more important of the two, so that efficiency often takes second priority until the desired level of reliability is reached. In many designs, higher output is important, but preventing failure is even more important.

In software, for example, while efficiency is desirable, designers warn that it should never be sought at the expense of reliability. In the design of bridges, buildings, dams, integrated circuits, spacecrafts, communications systems and so on, reliability is at the top of the list of design criteria, above or beside efficiency.

Is this debate applicable to economics?

Economies today are as much a product of social engineering and conscious design as they are a result of unplanned evolutionary development. Thus, it makes sense to review the lessons of engineering and systems design and ask whether these disciplines may offer useful insights for economic policy and decision-making.

Economies are systems with feedback and will therefore benefit from the insights of feedback theory. Economies are complex systems which occasionally fail. They can learn not only from the systems designers who have successfully engineered extremely complex but highly reliable hardware as well as software systems, but also from the lessons of systems which have failed miserably. It is as much from these failures as from the successes in minimizing the risk of failure that designers have extracted their heuristics for successful systems design.

It is now acknowledged, for instance, that many pre-industrial communities tend to minimize risk when optimizing their resources. This clashes with the approach of modern corporations, which would optimize these same resources by maximizing gain. We can expect that the optimum level of resource-use from the gain-maximizing firm's viewpoint will tend to be higher than the optimum level from the risk-minimizing communities' viewpoint. Thus, firms and other gain-maximizers may consider the local resources under-utilized, while the communities themselves consider their resources already optimally-used. This explains why resource conflicts between corporations and communities are so common in the countryside.

Improving reliability: the modular approach

The standard approach in designing for reliability is called modularization, i.e., break up the complex system into subsystems which are relatively independent from each other and which interact with each other only through well-defined, carefully-designed interfaces. Modularization is used both in hardware and software design.

The logic behind modularization is simple. In a system of many components, the number of possible pair interactions rises faster than the increase in the number of components, as the following table shows:

Table 3: Increasing complexity

No. of components	No. of possible pair interactions
1	0
2	1
3	3
4	6
5	10
6	15
7	21
8	28
9	36
10	45
100	4,950
1,000	499,500
10,000	49,995,000
N	N*(N-1)/2

The last line computes the number of combinations possible from N items taken two at a time. As the table shows, a larger system with ten times more components can be a hundred times more complex than a smaller system. As the number of possible interactions increase, it becomes increasingly more difficult to anticipate, trace or control the consequences of the interactions. Mutually-dampening interactions (negative feedback) will tend to stabilize the system. But mutually-reinforcing interactions (positive feedback) can result in oscillatory behavior or exponential growth. In physical systems, such instabilities can lead to breakdown.

In short, the risk of failure rises quickly as the number of components in a system increases. The purpose of modularization, therefore, is to keep the number of possible interactions to a manageable level, so that their consequences can be anticipated, monitored and controlled.

Modularizing a complex system

A system with 10,000 components, as the preceding table shows, will have 49,995,000 possible interactions between pairs of components. The challenge of design is how to reduce this number of interactions.

Applying the modular approach, this system may, for instance, be decomposed into a hypothetical 100x100 two-level system of 100 subsystems of 100 components each. (Obviously, real solutions don't decompose so cleanly.) Each subsystem will have 4,950 possible interactions. There are 101 modules – the main system of 100 interacting subsystems, and the 100 subsystems with 100 components each. So the total number of possible interactions will be (1+100) x 4,950 or 499,950, down from the original 49,995,000. By using modular design, we have reduced potential system complexity – and any risk of failure – by a factor of 100.

If this is not enough, we can apply the modular approach further, and make a 10x10x10x10 four-level system (again, idealized for illustration only). That is, every subsystem with 100 components each can again be decomposed into ten modules of ten components each, while the 100 subsystems themselves can also be broken up into ten modules of ten subsystems each. Now, we have a four-level hierarchy of modular units of ten subunits and 45 possible interactions each. At the top, the overall system is broken up into ten subsystems. Each subsystem is again broken up into ten subsubsystems, giving a total of 100 subsubsystems. Each subsubsystem is further broken up into ten subsubsubsystems, for a total of 1,000 subsubsubsystems. Finally, each subsubsubsystem is composed of ten components, giving us the original 10,000 components. In all, there are 1000 + 100 + 10 + 1 or 1,111 modular units, with a total possible interactions of 1,111 x 45 or 49,995, down from the two-level interactions of 499,950. We have reduced potential system complexity and improved reliability further, by an additional factor of 10, or a full improvement by a factor of 1,000 compared with the original humongous 10,000-component system.

Note, however, that the worst case path between two components has also become longer. In the two-level modular approach above, the worst case is an interaction between two components on two different subsystems. Their interaction will now have to go through the boundary of the first component's subsystem, across the space between two subsystems, through the boundary of the second component's subsystem. The efficiency of the system has decreased.

The worst case path between two components is even longer in the four-level modular approach, with the interaction having to pass through several levels of modular boundaries. The more reliable system is also less efficient.

This creation of a modular hierarchy of subsystems composed of fewer component units is also called decomposition. In this tension between loss of efficiency from too much emphasis on modularity and reliability, the common rule is to err in favor of the latter: reliability over efficiency. This is true for software as well as hardware design.

Economists commonly respond to the suggestion that reliability is more important than efficiency by asserting that since the frequency of failures affects efficiency too, it can be included in efficiency equations and therefore be taken into account by efficiency-based economic theory. Such response, however, assumes what is being questioned: that efficiency is more important than reliability. If the suggestion is accepted that reliability is important, efficiency improvements will instead have to be expressed in terms of their effects on reliability.

Modular systems: improving efficiency

Let us consider the reverse process: how does one improve the efficiency of an existing multi-level modular design, like the hypothetical four-level system above? Efficiency is worst in the case of interaction between two components whose modules belong to different subsubsubsystems, which then belong to different subsubsystems, which themselves belong to different subsystems. Such interaction passes through six interfaces in all – three on the way up the module hierarchy and three on the way down. If this interaction occurs much more frequently than anticipated by the original design, the efficiency of the whole system may suffer.

To improve efficiency, one can modify the original design by adding a direct path between the two components, bypassing all the modular interfaces. However, if the existing modular design was already working reliably, the implications of this new direct path must be carefully studied, lest replacing the long path with a direct one affect the rest of the design. For instance, one or both of the subsystems bypassed might be relying for their own proper functioning on the signals from either component. If these signals disappear because they took a more direct path instead, the affected subsystem may not function as designed. If a thorough review shows that a direct path can be added without problem, then indeed such a change may improve efficiency without causing a decrease in reliability. Often, however, due to the sheer number of possibilities, a 100% thorough review is not possible.

What about another pair of components? A direct connection between them can likewise shorten a path and improve efficiency. Again, the whole design must be thoroughly reviewed, in case such a change will affect other parts of the system.

As one efficiency improvement after another is done, the possibility of overlooking a negative consequence of the change increases, and so does the risk of introducing a problem (i.e., "bug") into what used to be a finely-working design.

Or we can go back to a two-level instead of a four-level module hierarchy. This reduces the worst-case path from 6 to 2, improving efficiency by a factor of 3. As we saw above, however, this will degrade reliability by a bigger factor of 10.

As we make changes for the sake of efficiency, the number of new potential interactions increases dramatically. In a complex system with thousands or even millions of components, it will become impossible to anticipate, study, or much less manage the side-effects of every interaction. The more changes, the greater the possibility of unintended problems, some of which may be obvious but some can be subtle, perhaps showing up only under conditions that rarely occur. This degrades the reliability of the system, making it more failure-prone.

Dynamic systems are more complex

In software and hardware design, the potential interactions are choices available to the designers at the start of the design process. When the design is done, only the interactions allowed in the design actually occur during system operation. When a system is modified or repaired, a technician may implement changes which create new connections between parts not provided for in the original design. This is especially true for software systems, whose flexibility easily allow modifications to the original design to be tried and implemented.

Reliable, modular systems which are modified over time become gradually less modular, as changes create more direct interactions among components that the design had isolated from each other. These modifications will often introduce system "bugs," which may occur immediately, or only under certain rare conditions. A single bug, or an accumulation of minor bugs, can eventually cause system failure. As the barriers between modules become porous and more direct interactions between components occur, the reliability goes down, the mean time between failures shortens, and the probability of occurrence of the next failure goes up.

Design means realizing a desired function by choosing a smaller set of component interactions and implementing the selected set in the design's medium. This may mean mechanical linkages between moving parts, pipes between containers, conductive connections between electronic parts, software instructions to maintain a data structure, and so on. Once done, permanently excluding the rest of the possible interactions, the design can then be tested for problems and improved.

In the case of very dynamic systems like economies, the potential interactions between system components – economic agents, in this case – can occur anytime. The design is never done, so to speak, but is in continuous flux and change. The market may be seen as a huge switching mechanism which establishes brief as well as long-term connections (i.e., transactions and contracts) between economic agents. For such extremely fluid systems, the possibility of positive feedback and instabilities are therefore always present, making approaches which enhance reliability and minimize the risk of failure even more important.

Barriers create modules

Modularization provides solid theoretical argument for barriers as part of economies. Such barriers are the equivalent of a module's boundaries, meant to confine direct component interaction within the module and to channel interactions with outside components through the module's interface with other modules. Tariff, immigration and capital controls, trade barriers, import controls, etc. form boundaries that in effect minimize interactions between economic agents in different countries and enhance the internal cohesion of each country. Advocates of free trade and open economies argue that all these result in inefficiencies. They may at times be right. But system designers consider these inefficiencies the necessary cost of enhancing reliability and reducing the risk of internal failure.

The debate boils down to a conflict of priority: efficiency or reliability.

Unfortunately, the blind pursuit of economic efficiency leads gain-maximizers to break down barriers which separate the world into many economic modules. Previously, these modules were loosely coupled, in the interest of greater reliability. As these barriers break down, new direct interactions become possible among the different components of different modules. Some of these interactions are bound to be mutually-reinforcing (positive feedback), creating instabilities and increasing the probability of system errors and failures.

Today, globalization is breaking down more and more barriers to economic transactions, creating new direct interactions among components of different modules which were previously isolated. Some of these new interactions involve mutually-reinforcing events, reflecting positive feedback. Herd behavior among speculative investors is one example. Positive feedback leads to oscillatory behavior or exponential growth, both of which are indications of instability.

A system with a lot of positive feedback is an unstable system. Like software which has been modified to rely increasingly on global variables, the global economic system gradually becomes problem-ridden, unreliable, and crash-prone.

Instability is exactly what the current globalized economy is showing. Anybody steeped in the theories of systems design will say, "what else can you expect?" Increasing reliance on global variables (international institutions, global corporations, global infrastructures, etc.), breaking down barriers and creating greater interdependence between modules, overemphasizing efficiency at the expense of maintaining modular boundaries – these are common design mistakes which in the past have invariably led to unmaintainable systems and early failures. They are leading to systemic instabilities and threatening failure in the global economy now.

Modular principles provide solid theoretical backing for current arguments against globalization and open economies, from scientific disciplines which have shown remarkable success in designing highly complex but very reliable systems.

Complex systems: improving reliability

In addition to modularization, systems design has developed other approaches for improving the reliability of complex systems:

Information hiding: Little internal information within a module should be available to other modules, which should only act through the external interfaces. This is a theoretical argument against the economic "transparency" global institutions are demanding from countries.

High internal cohesion: Every module should have a high level of interaction among its members. This argues for giving greater emphasis on local instead of international transactions, internal instead of external markets. From the systems point of view, this is a theoretical argument for nationalism and other cultural mechanisms for maintaining high internal cohesion.

Weak coupling between modules: Modules should be designed for low levels of interaction, compared to the high levels desired within each module. This prevents a problem within a module from quickly propagating to other modules. It helps isolate problems when they crop up, making it easier to solve the problem. This is the direct opposite of the "global interdependence" argument in economic debates. It is precisely this interdependence which tends to make the present global system unstable and crash-prone, because a problem in one module can very easily propagate to other modules.

Minimize global variables: Global variables are system components which are "visible" to every module. Their impact is system-wide. In software, they are highly undesirable. Much more preferable are local variables, i.e., system components whose effects are felt only within the module they belong to. This is a strong theoretical argument against powerful global institutions and players.

These guidelines clearly provide theoretical support for economic protectionism, internal markets, regulation, and so on.

The argument may even be extended to the biological field. Recombinant DNA technology has been breaking down species barriers, allowing new biochemical and genetic interactions which had not existed in the past. Again, reliability is giving way to efficiency. As biological, genetic and biochemical barriers are broken down, new interactions become possible, some with positive but others with negative impact. Subtle problems can arise, and the number of these problematic interactions will increase at a rate faster than the number of newly-interacting components. The reliability of the entire genetic system goes down, and the risk of failure – a genetic crash of some kind – increases.

The emergence of gain-maximizers

It is reasonable to assume that people tend to pursue a mix of strategies, ranging from predominantly risk-reducing to predominantly gain-improving, depending on their own personal inclinations as well as the specific situation.

Adam Smith laid the theoretical foundations for the pure gain-maximizing strategy, when he claimed that individuals freely competing in the market and maximizing gain only for themselves are – though they may not intend it – also maximizing gain for society as a whole. In short, free-market competition makes the entire economy run efficiently. Since then, efficiency and gain-maximization have become the mantra of economics.

Reality, however, hounded the theory. Humans had neither perfect information nor infinite computational powers. They were unpredictable, error-prone, emotional, and fickle. They did not behave like pure gain-maximizers. Many were risk-averse. So the "ideal" economic agent had to be invented: a pure gain-maximizer who, competing freely in the market, would also make the economy run efficiently. This ideal agent is the business firm, also known as the for-profit corporation. This ideal agent is even recognized as a legal person, with its own bundle of legal rights and obligations, separate from its shareholders, board of directors, or managers. This legal person has one and only one motivation: to maximize profits.

Today, there are two kinds of players in the economic arena: 1) natural persons, who pursue a time-varying mix of gain-improving and risk-reducing strategies, and 2) the business firms, which maximize their gain in the perfect image of neo-classical economic theory. From an evolutionary ecological perspective, one might study them as if they were two different species competing for the same ecological niche.

Evolutionary perspectives

Business firms have become the dominant players in most economies; natural persons now take a secondary and often minor role. This suggests that today's economic system has been selecting for the pure gain-maximizers at the expense of risk-minimizers and others who pursue mixed strategies. Better rewards for pure gain-maximizers lead to an increase in their population and force even natural persons to behave like pure gain-maximizers themselves. Those who don't are considered inefficient and therefore economically unfit, and the system makes it difficult for them to survive. A theoretical construct by economists of gain-maximizing economic agents keeping an economy efficient has, in a way, created these very agents and a system that selects for them.

Evolutionary development needs a population to work on. In the past, we had a respectable population of economic systems, each going through their own evolutionary process. A failure in one system left the others essentially untouched.

Almost all the economic systems of the world have become so interdependent that they now basically belong to one humongous global system. The pursuit of efficiency through economies-of-scale and global expansion has reduced an evolutionary process to an all-or-nothing proposition. Unfortunately, its design is being guided by gain-maximizing, efficiency-enhancing strategies which make the system less reliable and more error-prone. A system failure will be a global failure.

Shifting our priorities

This paper suggests restoring the criterion of reliability to its rightful place above efficiency in the list of important criteria for socio-economic decision-making. This would be the first step in rescuing society and economics from the dead-end and possible catastrophe created by pure gain-maximizers. Reliability and modularization sit on the very solid theoretical foundations of the engineering sciences and system design. Hopefully, they can provide better theoretical guidance for the difficult socio-economic decisions that we must make today.

Reliability and risk-minimization are not really a novel idea. It has been known for a long time that farmers are generally risk-averse. Environmentalists have long advocated their version of risk-reduction, which they call the precautionary principle.

The proposed shift in priority among governments and social planners from gain-maximization to risk-minimization is not an either/or proposition but a return to a more dynamic balance between the two, with the higher-priority strategy taking precedence more often than the other strategy. Such a shift, this paper suggests, will move societies towards more cooperation, sharing, equality and stability.

Frugality, cooperation and resource-pooling

Risk-reduction encourages ways of coping with risks that recall traditional values which are disappearing due to globalization. These include:

More frugality, less profligacy: One way of preparing for an uncertain future is saving, whenever there is a surplus. Another is conservation – to use available resources sparingly so that they will last longer. Risk-averse persons tend to be more frugal; a risk-averse society tends towards resource conservation rather than profligate exploitation. The environmental ethic "reduce, reuse, recycle" is another expression of these ideas. Businesses also save when they create a sinking fund to provide, for instance, for bad debts or future capital expenditures. It is a way of distributing risk over time.

More cooperation and sharing, less competition: Another way to reduce risk is to share it with others who are similarly exposed. Insurance is a good example. People exposed to the same risk can respond better when they cooperate rather than compete.

Risk-reduction mechanisms are replete with the language of welfare and cooperation. Risk-reduction seems to encourage people towards cooperation, sharing, pooling of resources and collective ownership. It automatically implies a welfare society, which takes care of the weak, the underprivileged and the inefficient and helps them lift themselves up beyond what society sees as levels of failure. In contrast, gain-maximization very often relies on competitive approaches. In fact, according to economic theory, a competitive free-market is a necessary condition for attaining the maximum economic efficiency.

This contrast suggests an alternative formulation of Adam Smith's hypothesis: a society where individuals – who may only have their self-interest in mind – try to lessen risks to themselves will settle on a state of least risk to society as a whole.

More commonly-owned resources, less privatization: Responding to risks often requires resources which are beyond the reach of individuals, forcing threatened individuals to pool their resources together to respond to such risks. Social security is one good example. Thus a society working towards lower risk will probably expand the public commons instead of privatizing it.

More attention to poverty, less to average incomes, much less to exceptionally high incomes. A family that goes to bed hungry every night represents a failure of society that is masked if incomes are averaged. Such averages will hide the daily occurrences of such failures, and society will be unable to respond properly. A risk-reducing strategy focuses society's attention to those lowest-income situations where society has failed and continues to fail.

The immediate implication of a risk-reducing strategy, therefore, is the need to look at and to remedy the plight of those at the bottom rungs of society.

One bonus of a risk-reducing strategy is a heightened awareness of limits. As perceived risk nears zero, risk-reducers can more easily come to a realization that enough has been done. Gain-maximizers, in contrast, face no such limit, and will try to grow without end. One can say that their limit is infinite gain. Zero, however, is so much easier to recognize as a physical limit than infinity.

We know the damage caused by gain-maximization. We have seen how reliability and risk-reduction can lead to more desirable societal outcomes. Isn't it time to consider shifting priorities and changing our criteria for decision-making?

Part V. Alternatives: A Non-Monopolistic Information Sector

Information monopolies work against the nature of information. Alternative approaches exist or are possible which are in better harmony with the nature of information. Some of these are explored in Part V.

In software, the most well-developed and carefully thought-out alternative is free software, a concept which ensures the users' freedom to use, share, and modify software through a legal contract called the GNU Public License (GPL). The most famous example of free software is probably the Unix-like operating system kernel called Linux. (Chapter 24)

In rural areas so deprived of necessary information, a low-power radio station serving several communities is definitely more accessible to the poor and more useful for local issues than the Internet. (Chapter 25)

In genetic information, as stored in seeds and in DNA, the key is to stop and eventually reverse the ongoing corporate privatization and to expand the genetic commons. (Chapter 26)

Countries which want to take advantage of the benefits of the Internet may do so at a much lower cost through appropriate technologies, free/open software, genuine compulsory licensing, public access stations and public/community ownership of the information infrastructure. (Chapter 27)

A relatively comprehensive program for the information sector which the author drafted has been adopted by the Philippine Greens. The program includes recognizing the right to know, the right to privacy, the moral rights of intellectuals, and the freedom to share information, as well as protecting life forms from patents, implementing genuine compulsory licensing, setting up public stations, ensuring universal access and focusing on the best lessons of our era. (Chapter 28)

The global expansion of the information economy is, in a way, a leading edge of globalization. Alternatives in the information sector therefore necessarily lead us to think about alternatives to globalization as well. In the final chapter, I share some thoughts about alternatives to capitalist globalization, including socialism, fundamentalism, and my own choice: the Green alternative. (Chapter 29)

24. A well-kept IT secret

The information technology (IT) industry appears to be hiding a well-kept secret. The secret is called Linux.

Like Microsoft Windows or the earlier MS-DOS, Linux is an operating system (OS) kernel, a set of programs which link the computer hardware to applications software. It is more accurately called Linux/GNU because the package includes another set of system software called GNU. The operating system is the first program that greets you when you turn your computer on.

Superior to Microsoft Windows

Linux is superior to Microsoft Windows in many respects. It can do several tasks at the same time (multitasking); and it can service several users at the same time (multi-user). It has all the facilities for communicating with other computers (networking): it can be a workstation, a server, or both; e-mail is built-in; and it is Internet-ready. Linux can be configured with a graphical user interface, and a typesetting system. Unlike Windows which inexplicably stops every now and then (sometimes taking your work file with it), Linux machines run twenty-four hours a day for months with no problem. Ask any local Internet service provider (ISP): many use Linux, hardly any use Windows NT.

And the best part is the price: Linux is freely available. You can copy it from friends, from the Internet, or from one machine to another. Of course, if you want the convenience of having a copy on CDROM, you can also buy Linux on a CDROM – for a fraction of what it will cost you to get permission (just the

---

This piece appeared in the column "Second Opinion" in the daily newspaper, Philippine Journal, *on November 6, 1998.*

permission, mind you) from Microsoft to use their inferior Windows software on a single machine.

Government should use it

For those on a tight budget who nonetheless need to use computers, Linux is heaven-sent. There's no need to buy one license for each computer, or one license for each user. In fact, it would be downright criminal for a government to squander its meager resources paying per user and per machine-copy of commercial software like MS-Windows, when a better freely-available alternative like Linux is available.

That's not all. Have you ever heard of Unix? That's *the* operating system, the one which runs on all kinds of computers from lowly 386s to supercomputing Crays. Nearly all computer science departments in every self-respecting university in the world use Unix as their platform for teaching and research. The latest developments in computer science often make their appearance on Unix first, before trickling down later to other operating systems like Microsoft Windows or the Mac OS.

Linux is Unix-compatible, a virtual Unix look-alike. In fact, the only reason its developers can't call Linux Unix is because Unix is a commercial trademark. Many users actually consider Linux better than many commercial Unix versions.

Schools should use it

If all Philippine schools used Linux instead of MS-Windows, our students would find themselves becoming familiar with a truly world-class operating system, one which is used in mini-computers, mainframes, research institutions, scientific establishments, government offices and business firms.

Students and programmers alike will love Linux because its entire source code comes with it. If you've never written a computer program before, you might have no idea of what "source code" is, so here's a little explanation:

Buildings are built from architectural plans; machines are built from technical drawings; electronic circuits are built from schematic diagrams; computer programs are built from source code. The source code is what computer programmers write. When they're done writing it, they compile the source code to build the final program, which is what users run. Just as it is hard to remodel a building without plans, repair a machine without drawings, or troubleshoot a circuit without schematics, it is even more difficult – in fact, next to impossible – to modify a program without its source code.

Easily customizable

Microsoft doesn't make its source code available; Linux does. Microsoft source code is a tightly-guarded company secret; the Linux developers encourage users to distribute their source code and to improve it. Linux can be customized much more easily than software whose source code is not available. MS-Windows users have to wait a long time for an improved version to be released by Microsoft. Because its source code comes with it, Linux is being improved all the time by thousands of independent developers and programmers who volunteer their time and effort to make the software faster, more robust, and generally better.

Because its developers recognize that users have the freedom to use Linux, the freedom to distribute it, and the freedom to modify it, Linux belongs to a class of software called "free software."

Why aren't others using it?

If it's so great, then why aren't more people using Linux?

First, it has no advertising or marketing budget that even remotely compares to those of commercial firms like Microsoft. People usually first learn about Linux by word-of-mouth, through occasional industry reports, or via the Internet; so it is diffusing much more slowly. Second, Linux is somewhat more difficult to install than MS-DOS or MS-Windows. This is due partly to the higher priority Linux gives to power and robustness over ease-of-setup and ease-of-use, and partly because Linux is much more configurable. Third, more commercial programs still run today on Windows than on Linux. Thus, Linux users will for some time have a narrower choice of software applications than Windows users. This is, however, slowly changing. For instance, there are now several commercial database programs for Linux.

Despite these, Microsoft is scared of Linux – very scared. In November 1998, an internal Microsoft document was leaked to the Internet. Confirmed by the company as authentic, the document reveals just how scared Microsoft is.

The Microsoft anti-Linux document

Below are excerpts from what is now called the "Microsoft Halloween document." (Note: OSS or "open source software" refers to Linux and other free software.):

- OSS poses a direct, short-term revenue and platform threat to Microsoft, particularly in server space. The [benefits of] intrinsic parallelism and free idea exchange in OSS are not replicable with our current licensing model.
- OSS software is at least as robust – if not more – than commercial alternatives. The Internet provides an ideal, high-visibility showcase [and] dramatic evidence that commercial quality can be achieved/exceeded by OSS projects.
- Linux has been deployed in mission-critical, commercial environments with an excellent pool of public testimonials. [It] outperforms many other UNIXes.
- The ability of the OSS process to collect and harness the collective IQ of thousands of individuals across the Internet is simply amazing. OSS evangelization scales

> with the size of the Internet much faster than our own; Linux can win as long as services/protocols are commodities.

Former President Ramos had been too preoccupied with enforcing and protecting the Microsoft monopoly in the Philippines, serving in effect as local sheriff for the richest man in the world.

Hopefully this time, President Estrada will realize that, together with other computer users, the government is itself going to be the eventual beneficiary of free software that is getting better and better all the time.

Thus, the President should ask the bureaucracy to throw its full support behind Linux and the free software movement.

25. IT or AT?

This is a comparison of two technologies for information exchange – the global Internet and low-power community radio. The costs are based on Philippine prices, which should more or less reflect typical developing country figures.

In a way, the two contrasting approaches may be identified by the common keywords that describe them: information technology (the Internet) or appropriate technology (low-power radio)?

User one-time entry cost

The Internet: Zero for telecenter users. However, telecenter users will find themselves at a huge disadvantage vis-‡-vis other Internet users due to the limitations of computing without one's own home or office PC. For mainstream Internet involvement, one would need at the minimum a subscription to an ISP, with its corresponding fees, as well as the cost of a computer, modem and telephone line. With used equipment, one can probably get set up with around $200.

Low-power radio: Zero for 80-90% of the population who already have a radio set. For the small minority who don't have one yet, the typical cost of a small AM/FM set is US$10-20 which is probably affordable to all but the poorest of the poor.

Recurring user costs

The Internet: The minimum recurring user cost is around one US dollar for every one to three hours of use. The figures are

---

This paper was presented at an international training workshop for Asia-Pacific women radio broadcasters on "The Significance of Radio to Social Movements," held by Isis International on June 3-8, 2002 in Manila.

still going down, though gradually. Currently, Philippine prices probably reflect a fight for market share more than for return on investment. Often taken for granted is the annual cost of maintenance and repair, which can reach 5-10% of the equipment cost. In many areas, lack of spare parts can delay repair for months; unskilled or dishonest repairmen can make the problem worse. At times, the cost of repair can approach the cost of new equipment. Some laptops are so difficult to repair that they are in effect throw-away items, discarded once they break down.

Low-power radio: A radio owner's recurring cost, assuming a rural setting unreached by electricity grid, is simply the cost of a set of batteries (US$1-2) every few months. The cost is negligible where grid electricity is available. This recurring cost is truly affordable to most of the rural poor, many of whom are spending this amount today for their transistor radio.

Network server one-time entry costs

The Internet: To set up a network server involves much higher costs than a simple user. A small server on the Internet would initially cost around US$1,000-3,000 for the CPU, modem, phone line and the initial ISP subscription.

Low-power radio: A basic FM micro-power radio station would cost around US$2,000-5,000. A micro-power station would probably cost about as much as a high-end Internet server. An organization or institution which can afford computers should be able to afford a micro-power radio station. The big question mark is the licensing cost, a politically-imposed cost which does not exist for Internet servers.

Recurring network costs

The Internet: Recurring network server costs would include training costs, staff salaries, and connectivity costs (i.e., the cost of dial up and dedicated lines). Training and staff costs tend to be high, because of the very rapid changes in the technology and the high turnover of technical people. Connectivity may cost around $100-1000/mo. Since servers normally have to run twenty-four hours a day, an annual maintenance cost of 5-10% of the equipment cost must be factored in.

Low-power radio: Because the technology is mature and standard, training and staff costs tend to be lower. There are minimal costs for electricity and supplies, and no connectivity costs, although a radio station might want an Internet connection for access to more information.

Equipment life

The Internet: The life of Internet equipment is relatively short due to unusually rapid changes not only in the technology but in the standards themselves. This, in effect, results in very high depreciation costs.

Low-power radio: Equipment life tends to be relatively long due to mature analog technology and stable standards. The useful life of analog audio and radio equipment can easily reach three to five times that of Internet equipment.

Cost: conclusion

The Internet: Considering the generally high cost for user and network server equipment, especially if maintenance and replacement costs are factored in, the Internet will probably remain mostly a tool for the elite (i.e., high- and some medium-income sectors) for quite some time.

Low-power radio: This technology is definitely affordable to low-income sectors (those earning US$5/day or lower).

Impact on jobs

The Internet: Computers enforce the automation paradigm, which displaces labor with machines. New ICT-based jobs may be created, which may tend to pay higher especially in foreign firms, encouraging a shift to jobs in the ICT sector. However, these jobs are also subject to the automation paradigm and thus may also be replaced later by machines. Furthermore, those who lose their jobs to machines may be the older and unskilled workers, who are often poor candidates for retraining.

Low-power radio: Radio does not have the built-in automation paradigm of the computer, and thus poses little threat against existing jobs.

Local culture

The Internet: The Internet requires read/write literacy. Its full benefit is available only to those who are familiar with English. Knowledge of English is essential when one goes into programming the technology.

Low-power radio: Community radio stations will naturally adopt the local language, given their local reach. Radio is also very compatible with pre-literate cultures that rely on oral traditions.

Production of equipment

The Internet: Internet hardware, software and connectivity are mostly imported. Very few companies are able to make the integrated circuits that comprise the basic parts of most Internet equipment.

Low-power radio: Hardware for low-power radio stations are simpler and easier to produce locally. Local, small-scale assembly of equipment is entirely possible.

Source of information

The Internet: Bulk of the material on the Internet is foreign material. Due to the sheer volume of information available, there is always something interesting to be found. But it is less useful for getting specific local information.

Low-power radio: Due to its limited reach, low-power radio stations have little choice but to deal mostly with local material.

Potential reach

The Internet: The Internet's global reach may cover up to several hundred million Internet users worldwide. But this potential reach is limited by the connection speed, by Internet gatekeepers, and by the dominant Internet language of English.

Low-power radio: FM stations can usually be received by radio sets within the line of sight. This can be very localized, in the case of valleys surrounded by hills or mountains. The area of coverage can be wider where the topography is more level, or where the radio station is on a hill overlooking a wider area.

Best use

The Internet: The best Internet applications are electronic mail, mailing lists, information searching, and international or national communications. Its biggest plus is flexibility, which makes it possible to mimic various media, paving the way for media convergence on a single global infrastructure.

Low-power radio: Community radios are most suited to local information dissemination, for building local public opinion, and for strengthening local community. Where it is the only contact of isolated families to the outside world, a community radio that can receive phone calls from the outside (say, from overseas workers) has also been used to announce urgent messages to individuals/ families.

Interactivity

The Internet: Facilities for feedback, exchange and dialog are built in. However, it can also be used as a one-way medium if little importance is attached to two-way interaction. Internet response times are reckoned in milliseconds to minutes.

Low-power radio: A radio transmitting station is a one-way medium. But radio programs can and do combine technologies (such as incoming phone lines, beepers, text messaging, discussion panels, roving reporters with two-way radios, etc.) to provide feedback, exchange and dialog. Response times are reckoned in seconds to days (for mailed-in feedback).

Advertising

The Internet: Like television, the Internet is a very good medium for advertising. Besides full-color, full-motion video, the promise of immediate response through credit card purchases makes the Internet a much more powerful advertising medium than even television.

Low-power radio: Radio is only a passable medium for advertising, because it lacks the multi-sensory attractions that television and the Internet can provide.

Information goods marketing

The Internet: The Internet is the perfect medium for marketing information goods, which can be directly downloaded from the Internet and immediately paid for online with a credit card.

Low-power radio: Radio is a poor medium for marketing information goods, because it is not possible to selectively download information material from the radio; nor can the technology be used as a payment mechanism.

Sensory demands

The Internet: Multi-media gives audio-visual and even full motion capability. For high end systems, 3-D is now possible; the future promises virtual reality. The Internet requires concentration and full attention of the user. The Internet's full sensory feed may encourage passive reception and discourage highly symbolic thought and the use of one's imagination. The Internet is inaccessible to the deaf or the blind, although some special but expensive equipment may help the blind.

Low-power radio: Being audio-only may be a limitation. But it can also be an advantage. Radio may be enjoyed while at work. One may engage in other activities while listening. Because it has no visual input, radio can in fact encourage the use of one's imagination. The technology is accessible to the blind, though not to the deaf.

Health issues

The Internet: Health concerns include radiation effects from high-frequency, very-high frequency, and near-microwave emissions; the impact of video monitors on eyesight; and Internet addiction. A computer user stares at a radiation source (the screen) barely a foot or two away, and for many hours on stretch. As more and more, including high school and even elementary students, do this on a daily basis, we can expect eyesight problems to become widespread.

Low-power radio: Radiation from broadcast transmitters is also a source of concern, but the risks are less for micro-power stations.

Accessibility

The Internet: The communication channels and servers of cyberspace are mostly private space. Many of those initially set up by governments are being privatized. This means that any claim of a right to access to the medium can be negated by counterclaims of the private owners of the medium.

Low-power radio: The radio spectrum is a public space. Thus, the public has an inherent right to access and to use it. Today, however, this right is restricted by governments through exclusionary licensing requirements. This is often justified with two arguments: 1) the spectrum is limited, so its use must be regulated; and 2) national security requires strict regulation to guard against anti-government activity. Both are false arguments. Even in the largest towns, small cities and most of the larger cities, few AM or FM stations are active; many frequency slots are unused and therefore available. In many towns, not even one station is operating. Like radio, the Internet can also be used for anti-government activity. Yet, no licenses are required from Internet servers. National security can always be invoked anyway, should a server start engaging in anti-government propaganda. There is no reason why the same liberal policy for the Internet cannot be adopted for community radio stations.

Gate keepers

The Internet: The Internet is not as democratic as the hype. Gatekeepers exercise control over the medium. Such control may be invisible and unintrusive, it can also be absolute. Gatekeepers include standards-setting bodies, IP address authorities, domain name owners, communication channel and server owners, search engines, portals, mailbox providers, mailing list owners and moderators, and Internet service providers. Increasingly, private entities and firms, who are not accountable to the public for their policies and actions, are taking over these gatekeeping functions.

Low-power radio: Radio has its own gate keepers, such as radio station owners, managers and announcers. But the biggest gate keeper of all is the government, through highly restrictive licensing requirements.

New technologies

The Internet: The next major advance will probably be virtual reality – 3-D, tactile suits and other reality-enhancing developments. This will probably worsen the negative elements about the Internet we have identified.

Low-power radio: A new technology called spread spectrum will allow many stations to share a segment of the radio spectrum with minimal interference. This technology is an answer to the so-called scarcity of the radio spectrum.

Default paradigms

The Internet: The Internet is not a neutral technology. It contains built-in values and default paradigms. These include: global competition, automation and the replacement of workers with machines, subsidy for global players, US/Europe-centric, Anglo-Saxon culture, and high-tech advocacy.

Low-power radio: The built-in values of community radio include local orientation, oral tradition, community-centeredness, local culture, and intermediate technology advocacy.

Government attitude

The Internet: Most governments tend to embrace the technology. No duties are imposed; the legal requirements are minimal; no license is usually required to set up an Internet server. Following the lead of U.S. and Europe, governments often adopt the policy of investing heavily in the new technology.

Low-power radio: Governments are almost one in restricting, taxing, heavily regulating, controlling and monitoring the technology. A license is invariably required to operate a station. The legal requirements are difficult and often exclusionary.

Development agencies attitude

The Internet: Funding agencies actively encourage, support, and fund ICT projects. In fact, they may even pressure NGOs to adopt ICTs (as when they insist on emailed attachments for reports). They are working hard to extend the reach of the Internet and to protect it from authoritarianism.

Low-power radio: With very few exceptions, radio broadcast projects seem to get low priority. There is mostly silence on radio spectrum democracy, radio access rights, and universal access to broadcast equipment.

NGO attitude

The Internet: NGOs are eager to explore the technology. Many have embraced it and have invested heavily in equipment. An increasing number are getting their own domain name and setting up their own websites. While the advantages are real for NGOs heavily involved in international work, they are not so obvious for local NGOs.

Low-power radio: There are very few NGO advocates of community radio. They are usually discouraged by the very restrictive government licensing requirements and the little support they could get from development agencies.

Benefits to rich countries

The Internet: As the Internet expands, rich countries will enjoy a huge expansion of their markets for hardware, software connectivity, consultancy and other ICT services. By using the Internet to tap cheap IT labor and expertise in poor countries, the rich countries can minimize immigration and restrict further the movement of labor. The rapid spread of credit cards and e-commerce will also expand the markets for their non-IT goods. Rich countries are masters of ICT; they are in the best position to take advantage of the new technologies.

Low-power radio: To ensure 100% coverage, AM/FM sets can be produced locally for the remaining 10-20% of the population without one. Micro-power broadcast stations can also be produced locally. By enhancing community interaction, low-power stations can encourage the development of the local economy, and reduce outmigration. By encouraging local commerce, local stations are less helpful in expanding the markets of rich countries. Community radio merges better with the needs of agricultural and industrializing economies.

Proposed alternate approaches

The Internet: The government must spend less on Internet infrastructure and more on other equally important infrastructure. No special tax breaks or duty exemptions should be granted to Internet infrastructure. The government should embrace the use of free/open software. Compulsory licenses should be issued on essential patented and copyrighted material. Public access stations should be set up, and community/public control and ownership over Internet infrastructure maintained. Later, an Internet connection for community radio stations may be explored. Check the viability of a stand-alone VCD player cum CDROM browser (<$40) for low-cost information dissemination.

Low-power radio: The government should give priority to local approaches like community radio. Restrictive legal requirements for low-power stations should be removed. They should instead enjoy tax breaks and duty exemptions. The local production of AM/FM sets and low-power broadcast stations should be encouraged. A wider segment of the broadcast spectrum should be allotted for low-power stations. Ceilings should be established on transmitting power, and gradually reduced over the years, to allow more low-power stations to go on the air. The expansion of community radio to include some offline facilities for email and lists as well as other intermediate technologies for information networking should also be explored.

A challenge to governments

For a small fraction of the cost of building an Internet infrastructure, a string of community-run low-power radio stations in the countryside can provide the poorest sections of society with an accessible medium for information access that closely matches their information needs.

It is a solution so appropriate that one wonders why it is not widely used.

The problem is an antiquated, highly centralized legal framework which burdens potential radio stations with extremely restrictive requirements that keep access to the radio spectrum in very few hands.

If governments only allowed ordinary people to set up a low-power radio station as freely as they can an Internet server, then we can quickly see which technology truly meets the people's information needs.

26. Community rights over biological material: property or moral rights?

A lingering issue in the current race to acquire breeders' rights and patents over living organisms is the prior rights of traditional communities and indigenous peoples who had maintained the world's biodiversity and developed the thousands of varieties of crops and medicinal plants that are the targets of bio-privatization today.

Biological material: private property or "common heritage"?

Proponents of community rights to biodiversity generally reject the privatization of biological materials and processes, including genetic material. We know that such privatization tends towards monopolies.

One such form of privatization is plant breeders' rights, giving private breeders some exclusive rights over the results of their plant breeding efforts. A more monopolistic form is the patent, a statutory (i.e., by the State; through statute) monopoly granted to the patent holder for a fixed period, typically two decades. The GATT/WTO has strengthened these two monopolistic forms of bio-privateering.

One concept initially stood against this trend towards biological privatization: the idea that all biological materials and processes are a "common heritage of humanity." It says that the world's biodiversity are a public commons. No one had exclusive ownership over them, so they should be accessible to everybody.

This paper was first circulated by the author in April 2001.

However, bio-privateers twisted this "common heritage" idea and insisted that it only applied to naturally-occurring biological material. Material modified through intellectual effort should be exempted, they said, and the intellectuals who did the work should have some private rights over these material. With this argument, they justified plant breeders' rights and later biopatents. Thus, the proponents of bio-privatization enjoyed the best of both worlds. They had unrestricted access to the "common heritage" of natural biodiversity worldwide – located mostly in biodiversity-rich developing countries. They took these natural biodiversity and modified them. Instead of returning it to the "common heritage", however, they staked their private claim on the modified material and excluded them from the common heritage. Once the idea took hold that modified biological material should enjoy some form of private property protection, the bundle of rights and scope of protection attached to the concept was gradually expanded, from limited breeders' rights to the more comprehensive patent rights. Thus, more and more biological material came under private ownership or control, while "common heritage" materials like traditional rice varieties and medicinal plants gradually disappeared.

National sovereignty over biological material

Few developing countries had the technology to compete in this privatization game. So they changed tack and abandoned the "common heritage" concept in its incomplete form (applicable only to natural but not to modified biological material). Instead, they switched to the idea of "national sovereignty." Like other natural resources such as mineral deposits, forest resources, water resources, etc., genetic material became State property. Historically the king was the State, so this is also called the Regalian doctrine. With this development, bio-privateers who had earlier freely collected natural biological material for later modification and privatization now had to negotiate with the "owner," i.e., the State, for the rights to do so.

The Regalian doctrine in this case became a monkey wrench that undermined the plans of powerful countries to freely collect biodiversity and privatize them through further breeding and genetic modification.

Historically, however, the Regalian doctrine had played a very different role. The doctrine had been a colonial instrument to seize control of resources from the communities which directly maintained, used and relied on these resources. As countries won independence from the colonial powers, the ownership by the colonial State, established through military might, subsequently passed on to national governments instead of reverting back to the communities from which they had been seized. Even today, the Regalian doctrine is a major State weapon against local communities, particularly indigenous communities, who want to reestablish their rights of access and control over resources which had been seized by colonial States.

Furthermore, States who claim ownership or control over genetic resources within their territories can easily enter into profit- or patent-sharing agreements with bio-privateers like biotech firms, as they have done with mining and logging firms. Thus, the Regalian doctrine may delay but not necessarily stop bio-privatization.

Because of their bad experience with the Regalian doctrine, many communities are not comfortable with "national sovereignty" over biological material. They prefer a different concept, usually called "community rights" over biological material. However, the concept is not as well defined as the concepts of "common heritage," of patents and other private property rights, or of State ownership. For one, communities do not usually claim property rights over genetic resources they maintain and use. Private ownership over such material goes against the grain of typical indigenous culture, which is probably closer to the idea of common heritage. What they usually want is some form of recognition of their contribution in developing and maintaining the biological material over hundreds or thousands of years, with some bundle of rights attached to such recognition. The concept, however, has remained ambiguous and contentious. There have been, for instance, no clear and consistent explanation of the precise rights associated with community rights over biological material.

Should such rights empower a community or tribe to enter into an agreement with a firm for the joint patent ownership of medicinal plants collected in their area and commercialized by the firm, for instance? This would pull the community rights concept closer towards monopoly, because patent rights include the right to exclude others from using, creating or taking commercial advantage of the patented material. (This has led to the suggestion by Richard Stallman of MIT and free software fame, for instance, that the privatization of biological material is more precisely called "bio-privateering" instead of biopiracy. When a tribe and a firm both agree to jointly patent biological material and split the benefits, it may not be biopiracy anymore, but it will still be bio-privateering.)

Back to "common heritage": socializing privatized material

Perhaps, a better approach is for communities to say that since they originally developed and preserved indigenous biological materials for the use of all, they don't mind the rest of the world benefiting from these, and they are passing them on to the rest of the world. But with some provisos: 1) that all useful materials, living or not, derived from them are likewise for the use of all, and cannot be patented; and 2) that having made such an important contribution to the "common heritage of humanity," they will also feel free to dip into the world's storehouse of knowledge, including those which have been copyrighted or patented, for material which they find useful.

Such approach preserves the indigenous culture of sharing and extends it wider, instead of giving up their culture to join the market for genetic material as suppliers.

In a way, the first proviso mirrors a similar alternative mechanism in the copyrights field, appropriately called copyleft.

Copyleft: the freedom to use, to share and to modify

In reaction to the monopolistic nature of copyrights, anti-monopoly software authors have created a precise legal concept called the GNU General Public License (GPL), developed by Richard Stallman and the Free Software Foundation. GPL is sometimes called copyleft. Whereas copyrights give software authors the right to exclude others from using, reproducing, modifying or selling their work without their permission, GPL preserves the public's right to use, share, and modify the program. Software distributed under GPL can be freely used, modified, copied and shared, given away or even sold by anybody. The modified programs will continue to have these user freedoms attached to them, including the freedom to sell the program. Such software is also called free software ("free as in freedom," as GPL advocates are wont to say).

The GPL has proven very effective in protecting free software from monopolistic hands. It even allows free software to be sold, as long as the rights of others to give it away or to sell it at a lower price is retained. The best example of GPL-protected software is the Linux/GNU operating system, which is increasingly challenging the world dominance of the MS-Windows operating system.

The GPL allows material to be given away as well as sold, leaving the user free to choose which freedom to exercise. This is freedom in the widest sense. This may need a bit of explanation: why allow anybody else to sell one's work?

The idea is that the wide distribution of one's work is a good way to get recognition of one's worth as a software author, which brings its own remuneration – including financial ones – over the long term. Thus, authors of free software recognize the freedom of others to distribute their work, or even to sell it. As the work becomes less scarce, the price of sold copies would gradually drop to some minimum floor level reflecting the actual cost of copying, the medium and miscellaneous overhead. Many firms and authors actually thrive selling free software which others at the same time give away. Such are the mysteries of sharing.

Free software authors get their income not from information rents such as royalties but from salaries, consultancy contracts, training fees and other non-monopolistic forms of remuneration. They get paid installing, modifying or maintaining software and training others to provide these services. The more widely their skills are recognized (as when their works are more widely circulated), the higher they can charge for these services.

Free seeds: to give away but not to sell?

Is copyleft applicable to seeds and other biological material? That is, can biological material be protected with the equivalent of GPL, so that they can be distributed with a bundle of rights, including the right to use the seed, to modify it through breeding, to give it away, or to sell it? If so, then "community rights" may come to mean the right to attach GPL-equivalent protection to plants and animals developed and preserved by communities and indigenous groups. Free seeds ("free as in freedom") will reliably keep such biological material within the commons, consistent with the culture of traditional communities and indigenous peoples.

Today, farmers groups opposing bio-privatization generally want seeds to be given away but not sold. The concern is that allowing the sale of seeds could lead eventually to a situation where the poor cannot get seeds because they cannot afford them.

However, refusing to sell seeds can lead to an interesting dilemma, because the same grain can serve as seed as well as food. Consider, for example, buying a bag from one who sells grain but not seeds. The seller may agree, if the grain will be eaten or fed to animals, but refuse, if grain will be planted as seed. In effect, the seller of grain-as-food restricts the freedom of buyers to put the grain to whatever use the buyer might decide (like using some for food and others for seed, or even changing their mind and planting what they originally intended to eat). The seller may, as an option, make sure the grain is not viable for planting before selling it, but this can lead to a slippery slope of restrictive practices like hybrids and terminators.

However, the concern that selling it will make a good unaffordable has not materialized in the case of free software protected with GPL. Some sell free software, but many give them away. As long as the information freedoms (referring to both software and the genetic information contained in the seed) include the right to use, to modify, to reproduce and to share the information (and the seed), lack of money will not lead to lack of access.

The experience of free software has shown that this is so. In fact, the same people who sell CDs of Linux often give away the same software over the Internet.

The lengthy and unresolved discussion of community rights over genetic material and biodiversity, it seems, can benefit from the earlier but parallel discussion about authors' rights, which has actually been going on for several hundred years.

Learning from the copyrights discussion: moral rights

For some, community rights refer more to a recognition of the role of local communities in developing and preserving the biological material, without the connotation of property ownership. In this case, the concept will involve a different bundle of rights. What this bundle of rights might be may be gleaned from earlier discussions in the copyrights area.

In copyrights, two distinct bundles of rights are associated with authors: property rights and moral rights. We are already familiar with intellectual property rights of authors, which are rights that exclude others from reproducing or financially gaining from one's work.

Moral rights cover a different bundle of rights. They refer to "ownership" not in the sense of property, but in the sense of authorship. Thus, moral rights involve recognition and integrity of the work more than its commercialization. For instance:

- The right to be recognized as the originator of your ideas is your moral right. Plagiarism violates such moral right, because somebody else gains recognition (regardless of the presence or absence of monetary reward) from your work.
- If written material you did not actually write is circulated in your name, you can if you want assert your moral right to stop the circulation of the material until your name as author is taken out.
- If someone takes some of your work, makes substantial modifications to it, and then circulates the material in your name, you may likewise insist on your moral right to deny authorship and to stop the circulation of the modified material.

Is it possible that these are the kind of rights communities are groping for, when they insist on community rights over indigenous biological material? Moral rights, a well-developed concept in the copyrights field, will extend to local communities the recognition and continued access they are after over biological material they have developed and maintained for hundreds if not thousands of years.

Curiously enough, the U.S. refused to recognize authors' moral rights, long after it has signed international conventions on authors' commercial/property rights.

Monopolistic and non-monopolistic approaches

Today, the global debate on bio-patenting, plant variety protection and TRIPS is held separately from the debate on copyrights issues, covering books, software, video and audio materials, and similar goods. The two debates should be linked

Patents and copyrights are two sides of the same process: the privatization and subsequent monopolization of information. This trend is strongest in economies whose products are taking less and less the nature of industrial goods and more and more the nature of information goods. Thus, ownership forms over information have become very important. This is why the U.S. has only one non-negotiable item in bilateral and multilateral trade negotiations – intellectual property rights (IPRs).

IPRs are the ownership form preferred by monopolistic information economies. This form conflicts with the fundamental nature of information goods, which are public goods. The social nature of public goods keeps reasserting itself against the monopolistic ownership forms adopted by today's information economies.

Community concepts of free use, sharing and common access are in better harmony with this social nature of seeds and of information.

Learning from indigenous peoples' land rights

We should also learn from indigenous peoples, whose rights to the land are seldom a simple choice between absolute private property rights and absolute State ownership. Concepts of stewardship and usufruct abound, and a complex hierarchy of access, control, exclusion and ownership of land has evolved that also varies from tribe to tribe. Some lands are family-owned; others belong to a clan; still others are under tribal control. Some hunting grounds are shared with other tribes. Some grounds are sacred and are taboo to all.

Rights over biological material and information goods may likewise require a similarly complex solution as befits the complexity of nature.

27. Low-cost strategies for ICT deployment in developing countries

The distinguishing feature of the information sector of the economy lies in the nature of information. The unique features of this sector therefore are better appreciated by first studying the nature of information.

The non-material nature of information distinguishes the information sector from two other major sectors of the economy. The industrial sector is the sector of material goods which are non-living. And the agricultural and fishery sector is the sector of living goods.

While information itself is non-material, it may need a material medium for storage and persistence. The baby's sex is information stored in the doctor's mind, later copied to the mother's. Shakespeare's poems are stored in books, on paper and ink. Computer programs are stored on magnetic or optical media. [1]

The development of new information and communications technologies (ICTs) has propelled the full emergence of the information economy by making it easier and easier to transfer information from one medium to another and from one form to another. Digital technologies have further revolutionized ICTs, by allowing these transfers and transformations to occur with no information loss. With today's technologies, the cost of replicating information without loss is approaching zero.

This paper was presented by the author in an international conference on "ICTs, NGOs and Developing Countries" sponsored by Interdoc, AsiaLink and the International NGO Forum on Indonesian Development (INFID) and held in Anyer, Indonesia on July 19-24, 1999.

High start-up costs, near-zero marginal costs

From this, we note another distinguishing feature of information goods: while the cost of moving or copying them is approaching zero, the initial costs involved in creating new information or in building the infrastructure for moving and manipulating them remain relatively high.

It takes a lot of effort to invent a new design, write a book, or develop software. But the cost of replicating them, once they are developed, is nearly zero. It also takes huge resources to set up information infrastructures such as transmitting stations, telephone exchanges, microwave repeaters, satellite facilities, copper and fiber optic lines, oceanic cables, etc. But once they are in place, the marginal cost of information transfer through these facilities is nearly zero.

Because of this, ICTs are very often much more accessible to those who can afford the high start up costs, than to those who cannot, to the rich than to the poor. Yet, those who are privileged to have access will then enjoy much lower marginal costs than those who don't and will therefore be in a much better position to compete vis-‡-vis the latter. In short, the rich will tend to become richer, and the poor poorer. While there will obviously be exceptions, the logic of the information sector – with its very high entry costs and very low marginal costs for those who are in – will generally work in favor of those who have the resources, capital and existing infrastructure to take full advantage of the benefits of ICTs.

Form of income: information rents

Because of the high costs of entry, it is often those who have access to huge resources who are in a position to set up the facilities for full utilization of the technology. In terms of content and software tools, private investors who do so clinch their control through statutory monopolies like patents and copyrights, which grant them the exclusive right to use the resources they have developed. In terms of the communications infrastructure, the huge investments involved exclude all but a few huge firms, who then lease out the resource under their control to other users. Either way, private control over the software and hardware infrastructure enables the owners to extract rents over the information resource.

This rent-seeking system eventually extracts from the public wealth that is way beyond the cost of setting up and maintaining the system. The rent-seekers of the cyber-economy, or the cyberlords, therefore become the superfluous and unwelcome propertied classes of the information economy.

The Internet has in fact become the leading edge of the global information economy, the new infrastructure for marketing the information products of the more technologically advanced countries. It will facilitate the intrusion of global capital into developing countries, the extraction of more wealth from them, and an even faster concentration of wealth among rich countries and global corporations.

Part II of this book elaborates on a detailed critique of the new ICTs.

To be connected or not?

To some, the misgivings about the new ICTs are enough reason not to plunge into these technologies yet. However, the option to stay away from the new ICTs may have its own pitfalls. While one can argue that to use them is to get trapped in a losing battle; one can also argue that not to use them is to lose the battle by default. Is the battle in the information arena worth fighting, or are we being drawn away from real wealth – our ecological wealth, our natural resources, our cultural heritage – to be exchanged with virtual and perhaps illusory wealth? The answers do not come so easily. Perhaps, we need to know a lot more about the technology itself and to dip one foot in to check the waters while reserving the option to get out if sharks and crocodiles lie in wait.

If a developing country – fully aware of the pitfalls and traps that lie in wait – nonetheless wants to tap ICTs and continue exploring the possibility of bringing their benefits to its people, what then are the options available to such a country? This is the question we will try to answer in the rest of this paper.

Cost of entry is a barrier

A real obstacle to the introduction of ICTs in a developing country is the high entry cost of the technologies. In the Philippines, for instance, the following summarizes the costs of providing 51% of Filipino families access to different technologies: (data circa 1994-1996)

Table 4: Cost of technology, per family and for 51% reach

Technology	Current reach (%)	Cost per family ($)	Total Cost for 51% reach (million $)
B&W TV only	43.00	100	102
Color TV only	14.00	300	1,413
VCR	12.00	250	1,241
Cable TV	2.00	1,000	6,236
Telephone	6.00	1,000	5,727
Fax	1.00	200	1,273
Internet	0.10	1,000	6,478
CDROM/DVD	0.10	300	1,943
Virtual Reality	0.00	2,000 (?)	12,982
Radio	84.00	10	20 (100% reach)
Total			37,314

Considering the rapid developments in the field, some of these technologies become obsolete rather quickly, forcing those who have made commitments to deploy them into another round of huge investments every few years or so.

Responding to high costs

The introduction of ICTs is an expensive proposition for most developing countries. They compete for our peoples' time, skills and attention, taking resources away from essential activities like food production, health services, basic education and so on. Yet, the possibilities of the new technologies are also tantalizing, and many people sincerely feel that these technologies also offer some benefits and, properly deployed, can facilitate solutions to the problems of providing for basic needs.

How does a poor country solve the problem of providing for its people facilities which are terribly expensive? I propose a five-point strategy for doing so:

- Stick to the idea of appropriate technology, make do without the online frills, and concentrate on low-cost off-line technologies, which can bring in the most essential services;
- Use free/open software where they are available, because they take full advantage of the benefits of pooling together the intellectual resources not only of a country but of the whole Internet community;
- Apply genuine compulsory licensing where commercial software is the only option; GCL is an internationally-recognized mechanism that allows poor countries access to technologies on their own terms;
- Set up public access stations that do not require the ordinary citizen to pay a fixed monthly charge; and
- Work out a system of public ownership over the hardware infrastructure to minimize rent-seeking by private interests, which can lead to further concentration of wealth.

Appropriate technologies

Countries must practice extreme care in selecting the technologies to tap, identifying those which are lower-cost, simpler, and capable enough to provide the most essential services. Often, as Schumacher pointed out, these are intermediate technologies, which greatly improve on the old ways of doing things but are very accessible to poor communities because the technologies are simpler and more affordable. Schumacher's ideas remains as relevant as ever in the information sector.

An example of appropriate technology is low-power, community-based radio broadcasting. As the table of technology costs above shows in the case of the Philippines, this technology can provide 100% access and approximate interactivity with very affordable investments, while the more advanced technologies would require billions of dollars of investments every several years or so and yet leave half of the population unserved.

In computer communications, appropriate technology would be off-line technologies, i.e., technologies based on store-and-forward email and email-based services such as mailing lists, email-enabled access to ftp sites, Web sites, etc. Such technologies would be text-mostly, off-line, low-bandwidth, and low-cost. They would run over the basic POTS ("plain old telephone system") network, instead of requiring a huge and expensive network of dedicated data lines.

Free/open software

The basic principle in overcoming high resource requirements is to pool meager resources and then share the benefits with as many people as possible. This is exactly what free/open software does: it pools the intellectual resources available over the Internet, and shares the results freely with the rest of the world. The result is something dramatic, effective and reliable. Free/open software are equal to if not better than commercial software in terms of quality and reliability.

The most popular example of this approach is the Linux/GNU operating system.

A philosophy of freedom

Linux represents a philosophy of freedom. It is freedom that makes free software like Linux/GNU "free": the freedom to use it; the freedom to copy and share it; and the freedom to modify it, because the source code is available.

These freedoms are the mark of free software. A legal document called the General Public License (GPL) was carefully formulated by the Free Software Foundation, headed by Richard Stallman, to protect these freedoms while the protected software goes through the process of use, sharing and modification. Thus, free software can also be defined as software that is protected under the GPL.

Access to the Linux/GNU source code means a pooling of R&D resources, an approach perfectly suited to a poor country like the Philippines.

The source code of a computer program is the equivalent of the schematic diagram of a piece of electronic equipment, the architectural plans of a building, or the mechanical drawings of a machine. Once a piece of equipment, a building, or a machine becomes complicated enough – as most pieces of software are – modification becomes extremely difficult without the corresponding schematic diagram, architectural plan, mechanical drawing, or source code.

Microsoft doesn't make its source code available; Linux/GNU does. Thus, Linux can be customized more easily than software without source code. Microsoft users have to wait a long time for the release of an improved version of the software. Linux is being improved all the time by the Internet community, which includes thousands of independent developers and programmers who volunteer their time and effort making the software faster, more robust, and generally better.

Working in harmony with the nature of information

One of the key concepts in ecology is the idea of harmony. We must learn to search for harmony and to work for it, because the dynamic balance that it represents gives peace to our lives. Thus, it is now commonly accepted that we must work in harmony with nature instead of in opposition to it. For to conquer nature and to defeat it is, in truth, a self-defeating goal, because we are part of nature.

Information has its own nature. It is non-material; basically a numeric measure of resolving uncertainty. By its nature, information is easy to duplicate at little cost, unlike material goods which require significant amounts of matter and energy to go into every unit. As the economist would say, the marginal cost of reproducing information approaches zero. It is this nature of information which determines its social character, why people tend to copy it, to share it, to exchange it. As the mathematician would say, the acquisition of information is not a zero-sum game, it is a positive sum-game. To use a popular term today, sharing information goods like software is a "win-win" situation, because you do not lose what you give away.

Free software like Linux/GNU works in harmony with the nature of information, because it recognizes and takes advantage of its social nature. Intellectual property rights (IPR) like software copyrights, on the other hand, work against the nature of information because they create statutory monopolies that artificially create information scarcity, so that the privileged monopolists can dictate their price of a good that, by nature, is easily available to all once created.

Despite the power of Bill Gates and his fellow cyberlords, they will never be able to completely impose their so-called property rights over information, because they work against the very nature of information. The social nature of information will continually assert itself and people will continue to copy and to share whatever information they find useful and worth sharing. On the other hand, free software and its copying license, the GPL, work in perfect harmony with the nature of information. In the future, IPR will become obsolete and GPL and similar practices consistent with information's social nature will become the general rule.

When we work in harmony with its nature, software becomes easier to improve; its quality, reliability and usefulness rises rapidly. This is probably why Linux is superior to Microsoft Windows. It can do many tasks (multitasking) and service many users (multi-user) at the same time. It has all the facilities for communicating with other computers (networking): it can be a workstation, a server, or both; e-mail is built-in; and it is Internet-ready. Linux can also be configured with a graphical user interface. Unlike Windows which inexplicably stops every now and then, Linux machines run 24 hours a day for months with no problem. Ask any local Internet service provider (ISP): many use Linux, hardly any ISP uses Windows NT.

Linux, furthermore, is Unix-compatible, a Unix look-alike. Unix is *the* operating system, the OS which runs on almost every computer from lowly 386s to super-computing Crays. Computer science departments in most major universities in the world use Unix as their platform for teaching and research. The latest academic developments often make their appearance on Unix first, before trickling down later to other operating systems like Microsoft Windows or the Mac OS.

Social movements and non-government organizations (NGOs) should look beyond the cost effectiveness of Linux, into its philosophy of freedom in software. It is a philosophy consistent with their advocacies – a philosophy of pooling resources, sharing, and working in harmony with nature and with information.

Genuine compulsory licensing (GCL)

While GPL ensures public access to free/open software, genuine compulsory licensing (GCL) provides an internationally-recognized mechanism for public access to commercial software and other copyrighted or patented goods at lower cost.

GCL works as follows: whoever wants to use/commercialize protected material approaches*not* the patent or copyright holder, but the government for a license to do so. The government grants the license, whether the original patent/copyright holder agrees or not, but compels the local licensee to pay the patent/copyright holder a royalty rate that is fixed by law. Many countries have used and continue to use compulsory licensing for important items like pharmaceuticals and books, to bring down prices and make them more affordable to ordinary citizens.

GCL would legalize computer shops which offer copying of commercial software as a service to the public, but would require these shops to pay a reasonable royalty – usually 5-10 percent of the local price of the copied item – to the original copyright holders. It would allow the government television channel, for instance, to broadcast the Discovery Series, while paying a reasonable royalty set by law.

Also called mandatory licensing by some, GCL is for countries who want access to technologies but cannot afford the price set by patent/copyright holders. While this internationally-recognized mechanism was meant for the benefit of poorer countries, even the U.S. and many European countries use it.

GCL is an important mechanism which not only helps poor countries access expensive technologies on their own terms, but also splits the cyberlord class because small cyberlords welcome GCL while big cyberlords oppose it.

When referring to compulsory licensing, it is important to emphasize that it must be genuine, because the GATT/WTO agreement pays lip service to compulsory licensing but defines it in a way that negates its essential purpose by giving back to cyberlords the power to set the terms of the license.

What about hardware?

Even free software like Linux/GNU are expensive in terms of the hardware required to run them and the time needed to learn them, master them, and modify them for our particular requirements. These additional investments have to be justified vis-a-vis the competing requirements of our impoverished people, only a small minority of whom have access to potable water, medical care or a telephone.

Unlike information goods, hardware is material. Therefore, the cost of replicating hardware and building infrastructure cannot take advantage of the near-zero marginal cost that information goods enjoy. Hardware is therefore expensive.

To look at the options open to a developing country which wants to provide access to ICTs to its citizens despite the huge capital requirements for doing so, it is useful to go back to the information superhighway analogy. A government which wants to provide universal access to transportation services will have the following approaches available:

- one family / one car
- walkways, bicycles
- efficient public transport

Most U.S. cities have taken the first approach. This is unfortunately the default approach taken by many developing countries, which mistake cars for a sign of progress. This misguided policy is further encouraged by those who export cars and other transport equipment to developing countries. A common way of doing so is by granting loans to cash-strapped governments to enable them to engage in road-building sprees so that people will buy more cars. We know today that this approach is unsustainable even for the rich countries which can afford it. Resources will certainly not be enough to supply the raw material as well as the fuel necessary to provide one car for every Indian or Chinese family. Even if there were, our atmosphere will never be able to accommodate the toxic and greenhouse gases that will be emitted as a result of such an approach.

Despite this, many developing countries continue to consider increasing car ownership as an indicator of national progress.

The second approach emphasizes non-motorized transport systems like covered walkways and bike paths. To a poor country, bicycle manufacturing is easier than car manufacturing. It will require less in terms of a road network and fuel. It is, recalling Schumacher, appropriate technology.

The third approach is one that emphasizes public access to a commonly-owned resource that is too expensive to be acquired on an individual basis. It nicely complements the second approach.

While the three approaches are not necessarily mutually exclusive, it often happens that one option precludes the other. In Metro Manila, for instance, government transport policies were heavily biased in favor of private cars, resulting in a rapid increase in private car ownership in the region. As the traffic situation deteriorated and road congestion worsened, it became very difficult to expand public transport services as the politically powerful car lobby insisted on retaining the private car biases in the government's transport policies. Therefore, instead of improving the bus and jeepney system, the government took the much more expensive option of building overhead rail systems, which will displace buses and jeepneys and free more roads for even more private cars.

Had the government paid early attention to the development of alternative transport systems like walkways, bike paths and an efficient public bus system, middle class families would not have found the private car a necessity for urban living, and neither would it have been necessary to build very expensive overhead rail-based systems. The experience of Curitiba in Brazil is a good example.

Unfortunately, government are often drawn away from this enlightened approach by the attractive loans dangled before them by countries who want them to build more roads instead so that they can buy more cars.

An early enlightened approach can make it much easier for a government to provide universal public access at a much lower cost, than if market forces were allowed to rule and set the direction of development of services. Letting the "free market" direct the deployment of infrastructure would lock a country into very expensive options which are most beneficial only for the suppliers of the technology.

Let us now pose the question: what would be the analogue in the information sector of walkways, bike paths, and an efficient public transport system, the approach that makes much more sense, particularly to developing countries, than the one-family, one-car approach?

The hardware solution: public facilities, universal access

Publicly-owned, publicly-accessible facilities represent this strategy of resource-pooling and resource-sharing, a proven strategy among poor countries. This approach contrasts sharply with what seems today to be the dominant idea for introducing ICTs: "a computer on every desktop," recalling the "one family, one car" approach in the transportation sector.

These two contrasting approaches are as follows:

- public libraries vs. a library in every home
- public viewing centers vs. a television in every home
- public calling stations vs. a telephone in every home
- public access terminals vs. a computer on every desktop

The first represents a community-oriented approach that emphasizes sharing and minimizes cost; the second represents an individualistic approach that creates a huge demand for suppliers.

It is clear what strategy the ICT industry wants governments to take. It is also clear what strategy will be able to deliver universal access at a cost which cash-strapped governments can afford.

Unfortunately, many governments do not give this issue much thought, and accept without question the approach which the ICT industry is taking. The Philippine government, for instance, had in 1998 a project to install a public calling station in every one of the 1,500 municipalities of the country. The budget for the project was drastically reduced; instead, the government is relying on private telephone companies to install telephones, which they are doing, but mostly in urban centers, and the target is to install one in every home.

Public ownership of the infrastructure

Because the ICT infrastructure is very expensive, the effort to set it up presents an opportunity for collective pooling of resources by an entire community. Once the infrastructure is set up, it can then offer universal access, charging only enough to maintain good quality service and provide for future requirements. This is the rationale for public ownership of natural monopolies and large infrastructures.

Private ownership of such public works opens the door to rent-seeking with no time bound, extracts additional cost from users to support the profit-driven rent-seekers who will charge as much as the market will bear, and contributes to the further concentration of wealth in the hands of the rich. Because of the low marginal costs of moving and reproducing information goods, the information sector attracts more than its usual share of rent-seekers. Public or community ownership of ICT infrastructures can avoid this problem.

Conclusion

The information economy is growing at a phenomenal rate, often independently of the capacity of communities to absorb it, or of governments to regulate it. This growth is driven mostly by external global forces which, having intruded into our own societies, treat our country and our communities simply as fodder for their relentless drive for profit and growth.

Our agricultural, industrial and information sectors often work in different, if not opposite, directions. What we want is their balanced development and interaction, in a way that enhances the overall quality of life in our communities.

To be able to attain this dynamic balance, so that these sectors enhance each other and contribute to the overall health and sustainability of our communities – this is the challenge of the information sector.

28. Greening the information sector

Social movements are beginning to respond to the specific issues involving the information economy. An illustrative set of responses can be seen in the programme of the Philippine Greens for a non-monopolistic information sector (*Society, Ecology and Transformation* by the Philippine Greens, 1997).

The Greens see the information sector as very important because of its special nature: information is a social good and it can be shared freely once it is created; and since information is a non-material good, the limits to material growth do not apply to information growth. The Greens consider their approach in harmony with this nature of information.

The following are the major elements of the Philippine Greens' programme for the information sector:

1. *The right to know.* It is the government's duty to inform its citizens about matters that directly affect them, their families or their communities. Citizens have the right to access these information. The State may not use 'national security,' 'confidentiality of commercial transactions,' or 'trade secret' reasons to curtail this right.

2. *The right to privacy.* The government will refrain from probing the private life of its citizens. Citizens have the right to access information about themselves which have been collected by government agencies. The government may not centralize these separate databases by building a central database or by adopting a

---

This was part of a paper presented by the author at the international conference "Colonialism To Globalization: Five Centuries After Vasco da Gama", sponsored by the Indian Social Institute (ISI) on February 2-6, 1998, in New Delhi, India. See also Society, Ecology and Transformation *by the Philippine Greens, 1997.*

unified access key to the separate databases. Nobody will be forced against their will to reveal any information they do not want to make public.

3. *No patenting of life forms*. The following, whether or not modified by human intervention, may not be patented: life forms, biological and microbiological materials, biological and microbiological processes.

Life form patenting has become a major global issue, as biotechnology corporations move towards the direct manipulation and commercialization of human genetic material. Biotech firms are engaged in a frantic race to patent DNA sequences, microorganisms, plants, animals, human genetic sequences and other biological material. They are also doing all kinds of experiments in genetic modification to explore their commercial possibilities. We must launch strong national and international movements to block these monopolistic moves and experiments, and to exclude life forms and other biological material from our patent systems.

4. *The moral rights of intellectuals*. Those who actually created an intellectual work or originated an idea have the right to be recognized that they did so. Nobody may claim authorship of works or ideas they did not originate. No one can be forced to release or modify a work or idea if he/she is not willing to do so. These and other moral rights of intellectuals will be respected and protected.

5. *The freedom to share*. The freedom to share and exchange information and knowledge will be recognized and protected. This freedom will take precedence over the information monopolies such as intellectual property rights (IPR) that the State grants to intellectuals.

A specific expression of the freedom to share is the "fair-use" policy. This policy reflects a historical struggle waged by librarians who see themselves as guardians of the world's storehouse of knowledge, which they want to be freely accessible to the public. Librarians and educators have fought long battles and firmly held their ground on the issue of fair-use, which allows students and researchers access to copyrighted or patented materials without paying IPR rents. They have recently been losing ground due to the increasing political power of cyberlords.

6. *Universal access*. The government will facilitate universal access by its citizens to the world's storehouse of knowledge. Every community will be enabled to have access to books, cassettes, videos, tapes, software, radio and TV programs, etc. The government will set up a wide range of training and educational facilities to enable community members to continually expand their know-how and knowledge.

7. *Compulsory licensing*. Universal access to information content is best implemented through compulsory licensing. Under this internationally-practiced mechanism, the government itself licenses others to copy patented or copyrighted material for sale to the public, but compels the licensees to pay the patent or copyright holder a government-set royalty fee. This mechanism is a transition step towards non-monopolistic payments for intellectual activity.

Many countries in the world have used and continue to use this mechanism for important products like pharmaceuticals and books. Compulsory licensing is an internationally-recognized mechanism specifically meant to benefit poorer countries who want to access technologies but cannot afford the price set by IPR holders, but even the U.S. and many European countries use it.

8. *Public stations*. Universal access to information infrastructure is best implemented through public access stations, charging at subsidized rates. These can include well-stocked public libraries; public telephone booths; community facilities for listening to or viewing training videos, documentaries, and the classics; public facilities for telegraph and electronic mail; educational radio and TV programs; and public access stations to computer networks.

Another approach in building public domain information tools is to support non-monopolistic mechanisms for rewarding intellectual creativity. Various concepts in software development and/or distribution have recently emerged, less monopolistic than IPRs. These include shareware, freeware, "copyleft" and the GNU General Public License (GPL). The latter is the most developed concept so far, and has managed to bridge the transition from monopoly to freedom in the information sector. In the personal computer arena, for example, the most significant challenger to the absolute monopoly of Microsoft Windows is the freely-available Linux/GNU operating system, which is covered by the GPL.

The first step in breaking up monopolies may be competition. But competition eventually leads to domination by the strong and those who can compete best, leading us back to monopolies. Isn't it better to transcend competition and move further towards cooperation? This means a stronger public sector and sharing meager resources to be able to afford expensive but necessary facilities. In the information sector, this means building information infrastructures, tools and contents which are in the public domain.

9. *The best lessons of our era.* While all knowledge and culture should be preserved and stored for posterity, we need to distill the best lessons of our era, to be taught – not sold – to the next generations. This should be a conscious, socially-guided selection process, undertaken with the greatest sensitivity and wisdom. It is not something that can be left to a profit-oriented educational system, circulation-driven mass media, or consumption-pushing advertising.

29. Alternatives to globalization

Nobody can deny today the increasingly serious side-effects of globalization and the international and national policies that foster it.

Globalization has enhanced the power of large investors – their mobility, reach, and political influence – but has at the same time led to a further deterioration in the living standards of the population and the state of our environment.

This has rekindled debates about the process and intensified efforts to pose alternatives which are friendlier to both working people and to nature. What are these alternatives?

Socialism

This the social system that went kaput in Eastern Europe and the Soviet Union and has since been abandoned by Vietnam and China. In a way, the two remaining bastions of socialism – Cuba and North Korea – would make a very interesting study, whether people who live within their borders are better off and happier than their counterparts elsewhere. Behind this social system, of course, is the communist ideology founded by Marx and Lenin and extended by Mao.

Despite the major setbacks suffered by this ideology in the past decade, advocates have persisted and their voices continue to be heard both internationally and locally.

This piece appeared in the column "Second Opinion" in the daily newspaper, Philippine Journal, *on November 13, 1998.*

Green alternatives

Another worldview – or ideology, if you will – has made considerable inroads among social movements, emerging as an alternative both to the "free-market" policies and gargantuan monopolies of capitalist globalization and the planned economy and class dictatorship of socialism. This worldview is a reflection of the growing realization that:

- Global corporations are contributing greatly to the destruction of our environment. The government must intervene actively and screen foreign investments to prevent potential environmental, health and safety impact and to ensure that they instead serve community needs and national priorities.
- The community is the most important locus of human activity. It provides both the basic human need for social interaction and allows structures that are small enough to make genuine democratic processes practicable and participatory.
- Nature should be treated less as a source of raw materials for exploitation and more as an ecological home that humanity shares with the rest of the living world, all of which have as much right as human beings to call the Earth their home. Human survival depends on the conservation of nature, not its destruction. Technologies that destroy or violate natural processes, such as chemical agriculture and genetic engineering, should be avoided in favor of ecological agriculture and organic farming.
- Quality of life should be emphasized more than quantity of consumption. This is a recognition that human happiness is not contingent on high levels of material consumption and that nature is unable to provide all the raw materials and energy that can meet very high consumption levels for all.

- Cooperation and sharing should be more valued than competition, monopoly or compulsion, and for small-scale, decentralized approaches preferred over large-scale, centralized approaches. Big projects like huge dams and nuclear plants should be avoided.

- Non-violence should be elevated to a principle of behavior that is reflected in our relationship with fellow human beings, in our interaction with nature, and our program for social change.

- The positive lessons from indigenous knowledge systems should be retained and promoted as alternatives to the increasingly violent and exploitative ways of modern science and technology.

These ideas can be found in an increasing body of literature worldwide, reflecting a new thinking that combines principles of ecology, social justice and self-determination in a way that consciously avoids the excesses of both capitalism and socialism.

The best known Greens are perhaps the German Greens, because they were the first to gain entry into a national parliament, and they are again the first to actually win national political power, although as minor partners to the more powerful Social Democrats. While the German Greens began as a grassroots movement which incorporated peace, environment, and feminist groups, their parliamentary involvement today overshadows their original roots. Other Greens try to blend a mix of grassroots organizing behind issues and parliamentary struggles that is rarely seen in other parties. Elsewhere, many Green groups continue to give the highest priority to grassroots organizing and mass-oriented campaigns, including many emerging Green groups in developing countries like the Philippines.

Fundamentalism

In a way, religious fundamentalism is another response to globalization, with its own set of alternative prescriptions. This response hews to a very strict code of conduct that is presumed to have been laid down by an all-powerful God. It has clearly become the dominant alternative in a number of Islamic states. It also has its Christian and Hindu versions.

There are also groups today engaged in an armed struggle to win political power whose alternative concepts belong to this category.

The best and the worst

Personally, I am strongly inclined towards the Green alternatives. They conform well to my own set of deeply-held values and beliefs, and I feel that they confront best the mix of problems that faces humanity today.

Every alternative, of course, has its best examples as well as its worst, its most shining moments as well as its most shameful, its periods of kindness as well as periods of ruthlessness.

We are often told to "hope for the best, but expect the worst." Based on the accumulated experiences of the Greens worldwide so far, the best would perhaps approximate the Utopian ideal, but the worst will still allow me sleep without nightmares.

The latter is not something I can say about other alternatives to globalization.

Index